MAYDAY!

MAYDAY!

SHIPWRECKS, TRAGEDIES & TALES FROM LONG ISLAND'S EASTERN SHORE

VAN R. FIELD

Charleston ┃ London

History
PRESS

Published by The History Press
Charleston, SC 29403
www.historypress.net

Copyright © 2008 by Van R. Field
All rights reserved

Cover design by Marshall Hudson.

First published 2008

Manufactured in the United Kingdom

ISBN 978.1.59629.247.5

Library of Congress Cataloging-in-Publication Data

Field, Van R.
Mayday! : shipwrecks, tragedies & tales from Long Island's eastern shore / Van Field.
p. cm.
Includes bibliographical references.
ISBN 978-1-59629-247-5 (alk. paper)
1. Shipwrecks--New York (State)--Long Island. 2. Coastwise shipping--New York (State)--
Long Island. I. Title.
G525.F493 2008
910.9163'46--dc22
                                    2007048971

Contents

Introduction

Long Island, that elongated glacial moraine spanning the breadth of New England's southern coastline, has been wedded to the sea since European settlers first arrived on its sandy shores. From the massive volume of container ships disembarking daily from Brooklyn's hyper-industrialized waterfront, to the yachts, sailboats and tourist ferries that ply the island's quieter waters, the sea remains Long Island's economic engine, lifeline to the mainland and playground.

Yet before the advent of radar, sonar, satellite-based navigation systems and the assorted electronic aids that convenience modern-day sea travel, braving the Long Island surf to sail the Atlantic was a risky, sometimes even lethal, proposition. Like the waters surrounding Cape Cod—the Northeast's other great glacial moraine—Long Island's open ocean (as opposed to the relative calm and tranquility of its sound) is notorious for swirling currents, shifting shoals and similar life-threatening hazards.

Over the past four centuries, ships have been coming to grief on Long Island's eastern shores with depressing frequency. Nicknamed "Wreck Alley," Long Island has witnessed hundreds of sinkings, enough for it to rival Cape Hatteras, that other great graveyard of the Atlantic.

Mayday! Shipwrecks, Tragedies & Tales from Long Island's Eastern Shore profiles a small but historical cross section of the broken vessels that litter Long Island's seafloor. From steamers to mail ships, coal schooners and nearly every other form of sailing craft imaginable—including a significant number of submarines—this book traces a thrilling, dramatic, yet also somber history of destruction and salvation that has played out of the Long Island coast since its colonial days.

Although the reader will probably note several patterns emerging from this chronicle of maritime disaster, the stories selected were not chosen to conform to any theory involving the history of Long Island's shipwrecks. Indeed, a smattering of offbeat tales involving rumrunners and infiltrations by Nazi agents (among other nefarious elements) have been included to display the full depth and variety of incidents that have occurred offshore of Long Island.

The wrecks of Long Island have played an instrumental role in shaping coastal New York's character and culture. Read on to acquire one small window into their fascinating and harrowing history.

Long Island Shipwrecks in the Age of Sail

THE WRECKING OF THE *SYLPH* ON JANUARY 17, 1815

Submitted to the Brooklyn Times *by Horace Raynor, 1842–1920*

In the event of a war with the British or other strong naval power, it is unquestionable that Long Island is one of the exposed portions and would likely be the scene of active operations. During the War of 1812, the British blockaded Long Island, where small sloops would load up with the fuel of the day: wood. Both wood and produce were in great demand in New York City. With this thought in mind, a correspondent of the *Brooklyn Times* interviewed some of the old inhabitants about the War of 1812 to 1815, and among their reminiscences were the following about the British sloop of war *Sylph*.

The ship was rated at eighteen guns, was commanded by Captain Dickens and carried a crew of 117 men. Being a fast sailor, she was detailed to act as a cruiser and dispatch boat in connection with the fleet that was then blockading New London and the entrance to Long Island Sound.

Among the many stories of her exploits was the following, which occurred during one of her cruises in the sound. She overhauled and captured one of the Wading River sloops that had been bound home from New York. The sloop's crew consisted of two men and a boy. The men's names were Emmons and Hulse and both have descendants now living in the vicinity.

Late in the afternoon, after the capture, a petty officer and two marines were put aboard as prize crew and were given orders to have the sloop follow the ship down the sound to Plum Gut. Emmons and Hulse planned to have the sloop drop slowly astern by "steering wild" until darkness set in. They then brought out a pack of cards and proposed a social time, saying, "We may as well make the best of a bad dish of porridge." As the evening wore on, a jug of New England rum was brought out and a good time was had until the soldiers were too far "over the seas" to tell whether the boy was steering for the *Sylph's* signal lantern or, as was the actual fact, for the Long Island shore. Just before the sloop struck the beach, Emmons and Hulse quietly hid the guns of the soldiers, which had been left standing in the companionway.

About midnight, the sloop struck land. The soldiers had had too much rum to offer resistance when Emmons and Hulse turned the table and became guards over the soldiers. They sent the boy ashore to arouse the farmers. It was near Baiting Hollow landing that the sloop struck and the few hardy men there were soon mustered and sent to Wading River for more help. Long Island farmers were Patriots then, as now, and at daybreak a horseman reached Manor, whence another was sent to Moriches and at sunrise the whole country was aroused. Every militia man had his "musket, cartridge box and forty-ball cartridges, as the law directs," and those who had no horse borrowed one from a neighbor and rode for Baiting Hollow.

The *Sylph*, when she missed her prize, turned back but did not locate the sloop until after sunrise. By that time, the woods behind the cliffs were swarming with the farmer militiamen. The *Sylph* manned her boats and sent them in with orders to burn the sloop, but the hardy Long Islanders kept up such a hot fire that the boats were beaten off. The ship fired a few broadsiders, but the farmers were too well covered by the wooded cliff to suffer loss. This story is often told, and the *Brooklyn Times* correspondent got it from Captain Norton Raynor, who was born in Manor in 1810. His father was one of those mustering and bought one of the "King's arms" taken from the marines, which is yet in existence.

The *Sylph* was finally lost on Southampton Beach, and Deacon William R. Howell, who was born in Southampton in 1799, and died in East Moriches in his ninety-seventh year, was an eyewitness of the wreck. He told the *Brooklyn Times* correspondent the story but a few weeks before his death, and it is given as near as possible in his own words. "Tell you about the loss of the *Sylph*? I guess I can. I can tell it much better than I could if it happened yesterday, for I forget recent occurrences, but those of my boyhood are yet fresh in my memory."

The deacon had a remarkable memory for dates, and in that respect was more accurate than the average chronological tables.

She came ashore about 2 o'clock in the morning of the 17th of January, 1815. The day before had been a raw, cold north-easterly day, but the sea was smooth enough for the whalemen to have their "weft" up, which meant good surf weather, and their lookout in the "crow's nest" on the beach. The whalemen said that the wind began to increase soon after dark, and at 10 o'clock, it was blowing hard, but the wind was somewhat "off shore," so that the sea did not increase much until after we sighted the ship at daylight. She had pounded over the outer bar and brought up near the shore. During the early morning, the wind had increased to hurricane force and it began to snow soon after midnight, while the weather was intensely cold. The whalemen said that the men could have landed safely at daylight if Captain Dickens had not thought more of the honor of the British naval service than he did of the safety of himself and of his boy, who was with him. He thought, so the purser, who was saved, said, it would be dishonorable to abandon the ship, and be saved as prisoners, preferring to stay by her and hoping she would live it out and be succored by some of the fleet from off New London.

When I reached the beach at 9 o'clock, the sea was breaking all over the ship. Many of the officers and men were collected in the tops and groups of men were standing in the lower rigging. The ship lay heading toward the shore with a list to port so that her lower yardarms were washed by the big breakers.

The beach was thronged with the hardy whalemen, fishermen and farmers, but it was impossible, at this time, to aid the imperiled seamen. The hatches and companionways had washed off and much of the baggage of the crew and internal fittings of the ship had washed ashore.

Among the wreckage on the beach were chests, trunks portmanteaus, some whole and some broken containing quantities of the finest broadcloth and linen garments, writing-desks, watches, jewelry and I don't know what all. Under direction of the wreckmaster, men were gathering and piling up everything of value.

Soon after I got there, a tremendous sea came roaring in on the ill-fated craft. It turned her completely over and smashed the greater part of her into oven wood. A piece of the bow, only held together by that was bottom up and with the bowsprit sticking into the sand.

The sea, for a few minutes seemed alive with the struggling men, but each wave lessened their number by hurling them against the pieces of wreckage and drawing them under the seething mass. There was a strong "set" to the west and the wreckage and men were borne along with it almost as fast as a man could walk.

The people on the beach forgot that they were enemies, and used every effort to rescue the drowning men. Some, at the risk of their own lives, rushed in whenever a man appeared near enough and thus a few were brought ashore but of these some were too far gone to resuscitate. A huge bonfire had been built and willing arms bore the few rescued to it, where dry clothes, from the unbroken chests, were put on, and stimulants administered, but at 11 o'clock but three were on the beach and living, the purser and two seamen. On the upturned bow were still seven men clinging to what looked like bolts or treenails projecting through the planks and sheathing, and one who seemed to be fast in some of the head rigging. About noon, it was snowing very fast. So much snow had fallen and been blown from the land into the sea that it seemed to deaden the force of the sea to such an extent that the hardy shore whalemen started for their boat station, two miles down the beach.

Although there were many to assist in dragging the boat through the snow, it was past 2 o'clock when I reached the disastrous scene. Many of the seas broke over the men clinging to the upturned bow. One after another, they were washed off, until, when the boat was launched, but four were left, and one of these missed his footing as he attempted to jump for the boat and was washed beyond the reach of the rescuers. The three taken off by the boat were black in the face from the exposure but eventually recovered.

Those saved were cared for at Southampton until fully recovered and were then taken to New York and as the war closed about that time, they were released. The dead were recovered and buried all along shore, some even at Fire Island and Islip.

The purser, whose name was William Burlington Parsons, married the daughter of the British consul in New York, and was in the lumber business there for years.

Every acknowledgment was courteously made to the Southampton people by the British naval officers off New London. Some of the material saved was, under the advice from the attorney-general, sold as enemy's property and the proceeds distributed among those engaged in the rescue. After the war, the people of Southampton showed their humanity by forwarding such articles as could be identified to the relatives of those lost.

This, the old deacon said, "was the most disastrous shipwreck of my time, and I remember a great many."

1836–37: THE *BRISTOL* AND THE *MEXICO*

The winter of 1836–37 brought many immigrants from Ireland to our shores. It also was a winter for storms. The *Bristol* sailed from Liverpool on October 16, 1836, with immigrant passengers aboard, hove to off Sandy Hook on November 20. Captain McKown ordered the flag to signal for a pilot be raised and the signal gun fired, however no pilot arrived. The pilot's indifference to this ship as well as the *Mexico* resulted in legislation setting up regulations for harbor pilots.

Captain McKown ordered the ship to stand offshore. In the process, the ship got too far east. By 4:00 a.m., the winds increased and the ship was blown by a heavy gale onto a bar off Far Rockaway, known as the Rockaway shoals, about a half mile offshore.

The *Bristol*, a nearly new American ship returning from her maiden voyage, was manned by a crew of sixteen officers and men. The ship was carrying assorted cargo and one hundred passengers, ninety of whom were in steerage.

Those ashore, local fishermen, were finally able to launch a small boat in the evening at low tide. This was before there was any sort of organized Life Saving Service. They made two trips to the ship, rescuing thirty-two in all. On the third try, the boat was swamped.

By the following morning, all that could be seen was the stern post sticking out above the sea.

The American barque *Mexico* left Liverpool, England, on October 23, 1836, only a week after the *Bristol* had departed. It did not, however, arrive off Sandy Hook until December 31. The weather was stormy during the entire trip. The cold was intense in the unheated quarters below deck. The immigrants, who had to furnish their own food in those days, were unable to kindle cooking fires because of the high seas. They were about out of rations because of the uncommonly long voyage. The *Mexico* was not able to find a pilot in spite of signaling that she was in distress. With worsening weather, she had no choice but to stand off to sea. On January 2 she returned and attempted to enter the bay, but a snowstorm drove her onto the bar about ten miles east of the site of the *Bristol* disaster.

She was carrying 112 immigrants and a crew of 16. It had turned bitterly cold and the waves were constantly breaking over what remained of the vessel. There were just eight survivors, according to Raynor Rock Smith, who was the wreck master on the beach. He, his three sons and three volunteers rowed out and were able to remove eight people, including the captain, from the bowsprit.

Captain Raynor Rock Smith's heroic rescue was the talk of the day. The *Mexico*'s owner gave him a purse of $350, which he divided among his crew. On March 27, 1837, a dinner was given in his honor at Oliver Conklin's Hotel in Hempstead, at which he was presented with a silver tankard, suitably inscribed.

Wreck masters were appointed by state, and earlier, by colonial governments. Their function was to go to the scene of a shipwreck and take charge. Wreck masters were empowered to hire people to unload or gather whatever washed ashore from a wreck. These men were usually older seafaring men with expertise in handling surf dories. The government had a vested interest in the collection of import taxes on the goods. The remains of the ships and their contents, if not claimed by the owners, were auctioned and the proceeds went into the government coffers.

In the wreck of the *Mexico*, about sixty of the dead, all stiffly frozen, were brought from the beach, piled crosswise on wooden sleds and placed in the barn of John Lott at Hick's Neck until a plot in the old Sand Hill Cemetery between Lynbrook and Rockville Center could be prepared. The sexton of the church had to use an axe to dig the graves because the frost was 5 feet deep. Lumber for the coffins was furnished by Oliver S. Denton of East Rockaway. The burial plot, 30 feet by 161 feet, was bought by popular subscription. The coffins were laid to rest in long trenches. A few of the bodies were recognized and taken by friends to be buried elsewhere.

One story that has been handed down concerns the body of a woman found on the beach with a little child clasped in her arms. They were frozen so solid that they could not be separated.

Local residents subscribed to a fund for a monument to those who had risked their lives to begin a new life in America. Captain Smith said that money taken from the pockets of the dead was added to the donations to buy the obelisk. The white marble memorial stands twelve feet high and four feet square and is suitably inscribed. Barely discernible, on the north face is inscribed the following:

> *In this grave from the wide ocean doth sleep*
> *The bodies of those that had crossed the deep*
> *And instead of being landed safe on the shore*
> *In a cold frosty night they are no more*

The Reverend Nathaniel Prime, while writing a *History of Long Island* in 1845, uncovered the story surrounding this curious epitaph. The committee who superintended the work had been presented with several epitaphs that possessed more merit. The committee adopted this one because the individual who had written it had pledged a liberal amount of money toward the memorial, provided his work was used. "This truly, is one way of purchasing an inglorious immortality at the expense of the literary reputation of a whole community; and the word was, that the committee consented to the terms."

1850: THE STRANGE STORY OF THE BARK *ELIZABETH*

The bark *Elizabeth* was wrecked in a summer storm at Point O'Woods on July 19, 1850, at 4:00 a.m. At that time, the only lifesaving apparatus was located at the Fire Island Light, maintained by the Lifesaving Benevolent Association of New York and manned by volunteers.

The *Elizabeth*, a 530-ton sailing vessel, sailed from Leghorn, Italy, on May 17, 1850, carrying cargo, five passengers and a crew of fourteen. In the cargo there was a large amount of rough cut marble, a large marble statue of George C. Calhoun, silks, liquors, oils, soap and other miscellaneous items. The ship was newly built and the down east captain was Seth Hasty. He had brought his wife Catherine along on the trip to Italy.

The passengers consisted of Count Giovanni Ossoli, his wife Margaret Fuller and his two-year-old son Angelino; a young Italian girl named Celeste Paolini, who acted as nursemaid for Nino, as the young boy was called; and a Mr. Horace Sumner.

Margaret Fuller was a famous writer and feminist. She was one of the few women admitted to the exclusive circle of writers that included Holmes, Thoreau and Emerson. She had gone abroad to serve as a nurse with the troops of Garibaldi in the Italian campaign for independence. While in Italy, she fell in love with the younger Count Ossoli, who was himself a national hero. It was to escape the press, which hounded them, that they were taking a sailing ship instead of one of the new steamships.

After a week at sea, the captain of the ship fell ill and soon died of smallpox. The ship was at that time anchored off Gibraltar. The British refused to let a doctor on board and instead quarantined the ship. After a week with no one showing signs of the disease, the *Elizabeth* set sail for New York with the first mate, Mr. Bangs, acting as captain. Two days later, two-year-old Nino came down with the deadly disease.

After nine days of nursing by the parents, the boy was on his way to recovery. July 18 found the *Elizabeth* approaching New York. The captain (former first mate) asked those aboard to pack their bags, as they would be docking in the morning. The wind built up to gale force. He, being inexperienced, underestimated the ship's speed and by 2:30 a.m. they were being driven onto the coast of Long Island. At 3:30 a.m. on July 19, the vessel struck the bar five miles east of the Fire Island light. The second wave picked the ship up and slammed it broadside to the bar. The force of the blow drove the cargo of marble through the ship's side, flooding the hold. The waves were sweeping the deck, which separated the crew from the passenger's area. The crewmen brought the passengers one by one to the forecastle.

Through the rain in the gray dawn, the beach could be made out with figures moving about, beachcombers looking for debris from the wreck. When it became obvious that no one was making any attempt to help from shore, it was decided that someone would have to swim the two hundred yards and go for help. The ship's boats were smashed. A sailor took a life jacket and jumped over the side. He was seen to make shore. Another sailor followed with a spar. Horace Sumner, following their example, jumped in with a plank and was seen to disappear. After this tragic event, the rest decided to settle down and wait for rescue.

Carts arrived on the beach, but were used to load the exotic cargo that was washing ashore. Finally the Francis metallic lifeboat arrived, along with a line-throwing mortar. The men were unable to launch the heavy boat into the mountainous seas. They made several attempts to fire a line aboard, but were unable to do so against the gale-force winds. For another two hours, the lifesavers and the people on the wreck simply looked at each other.

Captain Bangs had the men fasten ropes to planks. The plan was to have a passenger on the plank and have it propelled by a swimming sailor, but the passengers balked. Finally, Mrs. Catherine Hasty and a crewman jumped in together to prove to the others that it could be done. After a long struggle, in which the plank turned over twice, they were dragged half-conscious from the surf. They were carried by the current a long way down the beach. It was not known if those aboard saw them leave the surf.

The captain continued to argue with the passengers, trying to convince them that the plank ride was their best chance for survival. The passengers would not listen to him. Finally, exasperated, he shouted, "Save yourselves!" and jumped over the side, followed by most of the crew. Four of the crew stayed aboard. By 3:00 p.m., the ship was breaking up. A large wave broke on the ship, springing what was left of the mast. It went down, tearing up the deck and throwing everyone into the surf. The bodies of Nino and the ship's steward washed up onshore a short time later. Two of the sailors managed to swim to shore. The bodies of Ossoli and Margaret disappeared. All told, eight people drowned. Margaret had written to friends expressing her fears of a sea voyage and of drowning. She stated that if they were wrecked, she hoped that they would all go together.

An interview was given to the Providence, Rhode Island *Journal* on January 12, 1908, many years after the wreck, by Captain Arthur Dominy, superintendent of Fourth District (Long Island), U.S. Life-Saving Service. Dominy, a lifelong resident of Fire Island, was an eyewitness to the wreck, undoubtedly as a volunteer lifesaver. Providence had been the hometown of Margaret Fuller. He told the following story.

Following the wreck, Margaret's brothers arrived in New York and consulted with Horace Greeley, who told them that he would stay in touch with Fire Island. If the bodies showed up, he would see to it that they were properly cared for.

The word had spread amongst the Fire Island fishermen that Greeley was on the lookout for the bodies. When two bodies were found, they were not in good shape to be identified. The fisherman who found them put them in his sailboat and went to New York. He went to the editor of the *Journal* and told him his story. "Impossible," said the journalist. "It has been too long since the wreck to identify any bodies." The boatman did his best, but in vain, to convince Mr. Greeley of the truth of his message. He was told that a physician had stated positively that the body that lay in the little sailboat was that of a woman. Margaret was the only woman who had recently been lost at sea in the area. The man's gold teeth identified him as a rich gentleman, for no seaman of that day could afford gold fillings for his teeth.

The boatman returned to his craft, wondering what to do next. If the police discovered human remains aboard it would entail long and unpleasant explanations and perhaps a wait. As he cast off and drifted down the river, the thought occurred to him to simply find a quiet spot on the beach and bury them in the sand. He went ashore at Coney Island and back a little way from the beach, in the sand hills, he buried them under the cover of darkness. Captain Dominy later asked the man if he could find the spot again and was told that it was impossible, for the area had few landmarks.

Most everything that came ashore during the wreck was stolen by land sharks and pirates, even the clothes of the poor sailors who were wandering around half naked. About $15,000 worth of silk was stolen as the dead were being buried. The little boy was buried in an empty trunk. His body was later reclaimed by relatives and taken for a proper burial.

The ill-fated ship had come ashore opposite the house of Smith Oakes. He, along with Daniel Jones, Fredrick Rogers, William T. Hawkins, Daniel Neman and Selah Wood, were arrested for the crime of plundering the *Elizabeth* and its passengers. High bail was set and they were held over for the grand jury.

At the wreck site, the U.S. revenue cutter *Mohawk* stood by as the first efforts were made to recover the marble statue of George C. Calhoun. After many tries, the statue was finally recovered in November. Only one arm was broken, and it was successfully repaired. It was eventually unveiled at the capitol building in Columbia, South Carolina, and was later destroyed when Union troops under General Sherman burned the building on February 17, 1865.

When the summer resort was founded at Point o' Woods nearly fifty years after the wreck of the *Elizabeth*, a bronze plaque affixed to a block of granite was erected to the memory of Margaret. It lasted about ten years before it was washed into the sea.

1853: TWO WRECKS AT MORICHES

The surf off Moriches doesn't look any different than anywhere else on the south shore. The bar runs offshore as it does most everywhere else. But for some reason, the Moriches area had more than its share of shipwrecks. In 1849 the Lifesaving Benevolent Association, under the auspices of the U.S. Treasury Department, constructed a frame house on the beach and equipped it with a galvanized iron lifeboat that was fitted with air chambers, hauling line, blocks, a breeches buoy and a Manby Mortar, along with six hundred yards of shot line, shovels, lanterns and other rescue equipment. Stoves and fuel were placed in the building, which was to be utilized as a shelter as well as a storage room. These stations were placed along the south shore of Long Island at intervals.

A keeper was hired to oversee the operation. It was his job to recruit volunteers to use the equipment in case of a stranding. There was an incentive. After they removed the passengers and crew, they were hired to unload the ship and protect the cargo. The association was made up of importers and insurance people who had a vested interest in saving the cargo.

At Moriches, the equipment was soon to be tested. The sailing vessel *Persian* was stranded in April of 1853 with 218 passengers and a crew of 25. Captain E.D. Topping was in charge of the rescue operation. The rescue team was able to remove all the people safely, including one who was so sick that he had to be lowered on a litter. Many of the passengers were sick with smallpox. The weather was too bad to transport them off the beach, so they were quartered in the boathouse. The following morning the passengers were ferried across Moriches Bay to wagons to be transported to the closest railroad station at Yaphank, Long Island. The train completed the journey to New York City. The cargo was unloaded from the remains of the ship and followed the passengers to New York. The lifeboat was in the charge of Captain Norton Raynor and Jonathan S. Robinson of East Moriches. The keepers were usually elderly retired ships' captains and did not go out in the lifeboats.

A year later, on July 17, 1854, the side-wheeler *Franklin* grounded at Moriches in a dense summer fog. She was a wooden ship propelled by both steam and sail. She was 265 feet long, carrying 150 passengers and a crew of 50. Among the passengers were 12 nuns and a parrot valued at sixty dollars.

Volunteer lifesavers, using the Francis metallic lifeboat that was stored in the lifesaving building at Moriches, ran a line from the ship to the beach and all day lifeboats from the ship and shore were pulled to the beach and back conveying passengers, mail, baggage and valuables from the purser's department, including cases of valuable jewels. During the night, the ship came over the bar and struck broadside to the beach. A "telegraph" line was run from the main masthead to the shore, and the cargo was hoisted to the masthead and then sent ashore by the "telegraph." One of the articles of freight brought ashore was a circus pony valued at $1,200. As soon as he was landed, the caretaker put him through some of his tricks to ascertain his condition and amuse the wreckers.

While the passengers were boarding the surfboat for the trip ashore, a mother accidentally dropped her baby overboard. Sims Havens, who had a beach pavilion nearby, was helping out. He jumped in and saved the baby. The mother was so glad that her baby had been brought to shore safely that she dropped to her knees and kissed Havens's feet.

The keeper sent a messenger to New York to inform the owners of the ship. The last train had already left Yaphank, so he rode horseback all the way to New York, stopping at Babylon for a fresh horse. The owners dispatched salvage steamers from New York, but they were unable to get her off. In the process of trying to free the *Franklin*, the stern was wrenched off and came ashore.

Captain John Lewis bought the remains of the wreck, removed the shafts weighing fifteen tons each and shipped them to New York. Captain Lewis had a barge built to hold them. These shafts were exceedingly valuable and had taken six years to manufacture. A proved shaft was worth more than a new untried one.

The passengers were transported to shore and then by wagon to Manorville, but were too late to catch the one train to New York. The local people fed and took the passengers in for the night. One passenger stayed away from the others and kept his face hidden by a shawl, under which he passed his food. A young boy grabbed the shawl and pulled it away, revealing the smallpox pustules on his face. Everyone recoiled at the sight. Smallpox was a dangerous and much-feared disease. Camphor was burned and asafetida bags were quickly hung under the chins of those from Manorville. In spite of these precautions, Franklin Muller contracted the disease and died shortly thereafter. Others contracted the disease, but in a less virulent form.

Captain James A. Wotten stayed at a boardinghouse on Union Avenue in Center Moriches for several weeks while overseeing the unloading operations. Captain Wotten later commanded the armed steamer *Fulton* during the Civil War and captured several enemy ships.

He gave his telescope to his landlady, Mrs. Booth, to show his appreciation. A relative has recently donated it to the Moriches Bay Historical Society (Center Moriches, Long Island, New York), where it is on display along with a chair and a cabin door that were salvaged.

Most of the cargo was successfully salvaged, except for some crockery and muskets. The muskets were supposedly packed in crates filled with wax to protect them.

The seven-foot-high figurehead of Benjamin Franklin was seen for many years on a lawn in Bellport, Long Island, across from the Episcopal church. From there it is believed to have ended up on Cape Cod. In about 1894, a piece of her bow and forefoot came ashore and was scavenged for the metal in it.

Forty-six years after the wreck, on September 22, 1900, Captain Horace Raynor wrote the following for the *Brooklyn Daily Eagle*:

> *The wreck of the steamship* Franklin, *that has been a noted landmark for pilots and coasters is now doomed. A party of Boston men with a diver have begun to blow up the wreck with dynamite to recover the copper and yellow metal (brass?), of which large quantities are in the machinery and wood work of the old ship.*
>
> *The wreckers have completely ignored the owners of the* Franklin *and claim authority under a customhouse permit, saying that under the United States laws any wreck becomes abandoned if the owners do no work on it for three years.*
>
> *The people of all the villages in this section regret the loss of the wreck, as it has been a memento for more than a generation, and also because it has furnished the best of fishing grounds for sportsmen and guests here for years. The first blast of dynamite destroyed fish by the barrel full. The diver said the bottom was completely covered with dead black fish, black bass and porgies when he went down to see the effects of the blast.*

Evidently, the engine frame was too large and heavy to be removed, because it was plainly visible and was well out of the water at low tide for many years. Before the Moriches inlet broke through in 1931, the bootleggers used it to get their liquor ashore. They had rigged an endless clothesline, which was used to transport cases of bootleg booze from a small boat to those waiting ashore. This was much safer than having to land a boat in the surf. Offshore ships were signaled by oil lanterns of different colors burning in an upper-story window of the abandoned old East Bay Hotel at Great Gun Beach. During this period of time, the bar at the hotel came alive on Saturday night, with the bootleg booze flowing freely. All traces were gone by daylight.

During World War II, the U.S. Army Air Corps had a target range on the beach near Moriches, code named Rose Range. The planes also used the old wreck as a target.

On October of 1956, the U.S. Coast Guard declared it a hazard to navigation because it was just west of Moriches Inlet. A navy underwater demolition team was ordered in to blow it up. In 1978, they came back and finished the job.

1856: NO SURVIVORS! THE *JOHN MILTON* STORY

The 1,445-ton sailing vessel *John Milton* of Massachusetts left out of New York Harbor on December 6, 1856. Her destination was San Francisco, California, with cargo.

After the discovery of gold in the California territory, San Francisco was a popular destination. Would-be gold miners had the option of walking across the country through Indian territory behind a wagon full of their possessions or taking a sea voyage that could last from 160 to over 200 days.

The size of the crew indicates that the *John Milton* may have been a clipper ship. It was a 14,000-mile trip around South America and up the coast of Mexico and California.

After arriving in San Francisco Harbor, thirteen of the crew were removed from the ship for mutiny, which constituted a hanging offense at sea. What happened is unknown. The ship left San Francisco Bay for the first leg of the long trip home. Their next port of call was Callao, eight miles west of Lima, Peru, arriving on August 10, 1857. After two weeks in port, she left for the Chincha Islands off Peru to pick up a cargo of guano.

The next port of call was Hampton Roads, Virginia, where she arrived on February 14. After taking on supplies for the rest of the trip to Boston, the crew put to sea on February 16 with light and favorable breezes. On February 17 the following was recorded in the log. "Strong winds, double reef topsails, latter part strong winds and thick snowstorm." The last entry on Thursday, February 18 told of continuing gales and snow, then later in the day it was recorded that the weather had moderated somewhat and they were able to take a bearing. They were at thirty-six degrees fifty-six minutes, which put them off Cape May, New Jersey. The weather turned bad again and there were no more entries in the log, probably because the captain was too busy attempting to sail his ship through the snowstorm.

Sometime Friday night or early Saturday morning the *John Milton* sailed directly into the rocks at Montauk, about five miles west of the Montauk Point lighthouse. The ship's longboat was discovered ashore by a member of the Straton family from the "third" house nearby and was the first indication of the wreck. It was found with a bag stuffed up in the bow with a ship's compass, a bag of hard tack, the ship's log book, chronometer and various other things useful to shipwrecked sailors.

Soon the frozen bodies started to wash up on the beach along with debris from the ship. Dr. Abel Huntington, a young boy in 1858, was witness to the events that followed. He recounted his experience thirty-two years later:

> *I can recall distinctly the northeast snowstorm which set in on the 19ᵗʰ of February, and how thick the air was with the driving snow amid which, on the morning of the 20ᵗʰ, just before day, the ship, with close reefed sails topsails, dashed to her fate, and every one of the twenty seven souls aboard were plunged to death in the icy waves or crushed by the falling mass of spars and cordage, as by the suddenness of the shock everything went by the board and the great hulk itself parted in twain.*
>
> *My father was Coroner at the time and I recollect how a messenger came on horseback the next morning, bringing from Montauk news of the fearful wreck and loss of life; and later, just as the dusk of twilight gathered 'round, how two farm wagons rolled slowly through the snow up to our home and fourteen frozen corpses were lifted out and laid side by side in the carriage house. I remember also, with what feelings of awe I went with my father later in the evening and gazed by the light of a dimly burning lantern on the ghastly spectacle. For days afterward the remaining bodies of the crew were brought by twos and threes as they were found along the shore, until at last on the second Sabbath following the wreck, the great funeral service was held in the old church which was then the place of worship in East Hampton. Rev. Mr. Mershon preached the discourse to a densely packed audience, and at its close an immense cortege moved to the cemetery at the south end of the long street, where the interment took place, and where the monument now stands.*

The bodies were buried in a common grave. The whole town attended the funeral, and a stone was erected by public subscription. At the time, Reverend Mershon was criticized for conducting Presbyterian funeral services for those whose religious convictions were unknown.

The ship's bell was recovered and presented to the East Hampton Presbyterian Church by the ship's owners. It was installed in the

Session House (Sunday school building). The bell was damaged in the 1938 hurricane. After repairs, it again resided in the bell tower until 1976, when it was removed and placed on display in the sanctuary of the Session House. It remains there today.

One account had thirty-three lost and Dr. Huntington recorded twenty-seven. As the ship was returning from a two-year trip, some members may have been lost before this wreck or others may have never been recovered.

Some two weeks after the wreck, Mr. Aleck Gould was walking the beach when he discovered a sailor's pea coat partially buried in the sand. While putting it on a piece of driftwood to dry, he noticed that it was unusually heavy. He checked the pockets and found over $400 in gold coins. Being an honest man, he turned the gold over to the coroner. It was afterward found to be the coat of the captain, Ephraim Harding. The gold was later turned over to the captain's widow. The coat was found with one of the sleeves turned inside out, as though the owner had shed it while in the water. The captain's son, who was about twenty, also perished in the shipwreck. The captain's body was picked up by the family.

Old seafaring men reckoned the new light at Shinnecock may have confused those on the ship. It went into use January 1, 1858, and was given a steady light, which had always been Montauk's identifier. Montauk's light was changed to flashing. Ships returning from long voyages had no way of knowing of the change. It seems that it would have been prudent to have left Montauk alone and assigned a new identification to Shinnecock. The distance from the Shinnecock light to the crash site is about the same distance the ship would have sailed after sighting the Montauk light to make the turn into Block Island Sound, just where the captain was probably heading.

That same year the whaler *Washington* was headed for Sag Harbor after three years in the Pacific. After spotting the steady light at night, the captain became confused because his reckoning put him west of Montauk. The ship's company all declared it had to be Montauk because there was no other light like it on the coast and they were anxious to get home. The captain held out until morning and was certainly glad he did!

Tragic events such as this were often immortalized in poetry. This poem was published years after the event.

A Reminiscence of the lost ship John Milton
by Dr. A. Huntington, Brooklyn, NY, Feb. 15, 1890

How sweetly now the moonbeams sleep
Upon the ocean's heaving breast;
Where erst the storm with mad'ning leap,
Swept icily from crest to crest.

How soft the waves break on the shore,
Scarce ruffled by a zephyr's breath;
Where once, with grinding plunge and roar,
They dashed the sailor to his death.

What night of horror when that barque,
Swift cutting thro' the snow wreathed gloom;
like arrow to its destined mark
Sped headlong to her fearful doom.

But now beneath the silver sheen,
sleep placidly the murmuring waves;
No sign to mark the spot is seen
Where stalwart men found watery graves.

But like the reef of "Norman's Woe,"
Where sank the "Hesperus" of old;
So of this spot, 'mid night and snow,
Shall the sad "Milton's" fate be told.

Long Island Shipwrecks in the Age of Steam

THE WRECK OF THE *CIRCASSIAN*, A STEAMER TURNED SAILING SHIP

This is a story of a tragedy that did not have to be, except for the stubbornness of one man.

The ship was 280 feet long, 1,741 tons burden and twenty years old at the time of the disaster. She started out as a steamer owned by British shippers. During the Civil War the *Somerset*, a converted Fulton ferryboat, captured her as a blockade runner from the North in the Gulf of Mexico.

She was sold to American interests in the North. A short time later she went aground at Sable Island. The Colombian Wrecking Company got her off. In the process, Captain John Lewis of the wrecking company lost his life. She was resold and purchased by a New York firm and put on a New Orleans to New York run. She ran aground again at Squan, New Jersey, in December of 1869. She was gotten off and tied up at a dock for three years. She was then sold to a firm in Liverpool, England, which converted her to a three-masted, iron-hulled sailing vessel.

Her last fateful voyage from Liverpool to New York was with a crew of thirty-seven persons. She had picked up twelve additional passengers taken from a shipwreck at sea.

It was difficult to hire a crew because the sailors considered her a jinxed ship. Her bad luck continued when on December 11, 1876, shortly before 11:00 p.m., she ran up on a bar in a northeast gale accompanied by a blinding snowstorm.

Just four years earlier, the U.S. Life-Saving Service had started hiring regular surfmen to serve during the winter season. The stranding occurred near the Mecox (Bridgehampton) Life-Saving Station and the lifesavers were soon on scene. They dragged their heavy metallic Francis lifeboat to the scene. The old Francis lifeboats had been issued in 1849 when the first volunteer lifesaving stations were built on Long Island. Their new Beebe surfboat had been loaned to the Philadelphia Centennial Exposition for a lifesaving display and had not arrived back yet.

Captain Baldwin Cook decided to wait until morning to remove the crew. Meanwhile, he requested aid from the adjacent Southampton and Georgica Life Saving Stations.

On this Monday morning, the winter term of the Bridgehampton Literary and Commercial Institute was to begin. In the words of William D. Halsey, a young boy who was due to start a new term at school, "Was there a school session that morning? I should say not!" Every student was on the beach, along with most of the residents. This was a show too good to miss.

Lifesaving stations from Southampton east to Montauk had no bay; the ocean beach was just a short distance out of town. Captain Baldwin Cook made several attempts to launch into the rough surf. At 11:00 a.m., he was finally successful. Captain Cook was the last to jump into the boat, but his bulky cork life jacket got caught on the long tubular fender that was wrapped around the boat at the gunwale. He could not get into the boat but clung to the side. As soon as the crew cleared the breakers, two of them hauled the keeper aboard.

They brought a couple of ship's officers off and they went immediately to the telegraph office to telegraph the ship's agents in New York. A wrecking tug with lighters soon arrived and began work trying to dislodge the ship. The lifesavers no doubt headed for shelter and some dry clothing. Captain Henry E. Huntting, who was superintendent of lifesaving stations on Long Island, was on hand, as he lived nearby.

The next day all hands were brought ashore through the heavy surf. It took seven trips. The vessel was then turned over to the Coast Wrecking Company, which put on board twelve local workers who they had just recruited, ten of whom were Shinnecock Indians. Sixteen of the regular crew were returned, along with Captain John Lewis, a former skipper of the ship now in the employ of the wrecking company.

Captain Luther Burnett, a man with much experience in small boat handling, was hired by the Coast Wrecking Company to take charge of bringing the cargo ashore as it was being taken from the hold of the ship by the work crew aboard. For some unexplained reason, the crew unloaded the middle cargo hold first, leaving the fore and aft holds to be unloaded later. This put a great strain on the hull of the ship, as it was resting with the sandbar under the middle of the ship with the bow and stern both in deeper water.

The wrecking company went to work setting heavy anchors offshore and running line to the capstans aboard, which were used to keep the line taut. As the ship rolled in the surf, some of the men aboard would take a turn on the capstan. This was a method used to gradually help to work the ship off the bar. Over a two-week period they managed to move the ship 98 yards. This left her 308 yards from shore at low tide.

The wrecking captain soon got the storm that he was waiting for to float the ship free. The storm built for three days and by December 29 the storm intensified so that the small boats unloading cargo could no longer be safely used. Captain Charlie went out one last time to remove the cargo crew and asked to remove the others, but the wrecking captain said no, risking everyone's life on his gamble to get the ship off. He needed the men to sail the ship when she broke loose on the extra high tide that would accompany the storm. He had the lifesavers' life line cut so that the crew couldn't get off the ship. He told everyone, "We'll float tonight or we go to Hell!"

By nightfall the storm struck with the fury of a hurricane. The surf was up to the beach hills and spilling over. The lifesavers needed a spot to reset their line-throwing Manby mortar. The only spot out of the surf they could find put them 380 yards from the ship, about

out of range for the gun on a calm day, and they had to fire into the teeth of a gale. It was almost impossible to keep the sand and salt spray from the shot line, which needed to be laid out so that it would not snarl when the gun was fired. They had great trouble keeping the taper lit that was used to fire the powder in the gun.

They signaled the men on the ship with a red Coston flare to let them know that their plight was known ashore. The capstans had been loosened in hopes that the ship might blow closer to shore, but this had no effect; the ship's back had already broken. By this time men had taken to the fore rigging for safety because by now the decks were continuously swept by great waves. The wind suddenly shifted from southeast to southwest, causing a terrific cross-sea action, which poured water on the decks from all directions. At the same time there were torrents of rain falling and the winds picked up and blew the sand in the faces of those on the beach. The wind shift caused the lifesavers to re-site the mortar to allow for the shift. Their efforts to put a line aboard were unsuccessful. Even if they succeeded, those aboard would have been unable to retrieve it from the deck.

At midnight the tide was low and some activity was seen on deck. The men left the foremast and climbed into the mizzenmast (rear), which was of iron. By 3:30 a.m., it was seen that the ship's hull had broken in two and the mizzenmast with its human load was beginning to lean to port.

Captain Huntting, seeing the ship breaking up, organized the surfmen into squads of approximately eighteen men and equipped them with lanterns. They moved along the surf line looking for any possible survivors. Suddenly a shout went up from one of the search parties and soon they appeared supporting four men who had made it to shore. They were rushed to the nearby station, warmed and given first aid. These four were the only survivors; the remaining twenty-eight all perished.

During the period of low tide, when the deck was comparatively free of water, the first and second mate of the ship's company, along with a carpenter and a seaman from the wrecking crew, found a cylinder of cork that had been part of a fender for one of the lifeboats. It was about five feet long and eleven inches in diameter. They fitted it with straps to hold onto. Their plan was to straddle this strange craft and ride it to shore.

As the mast fell, dumping its human cargo into the frigid waters, the four jumped together with their craft. Once in the water, they quickly faced each other in two pairs and locked legs underneath. The mate would yell for all to hold their breath when a wave was spotted. By holding their breath at the right time, they managed to drift ashore without drowning. The lifesavers waded out into the surf and dragged them in as soon as they were spotted.

Bodies began washing ashore the next morning as the beaches were searched. The townspeople whose families claimed the bodies, with the exception of Captain Lewis and three others, buried the men. Fourteen of the sailors were buried in the Old South End Cemetery in East Hampton. The Indians were transported to Southampton for burial on the reservation. A monument was erected there for them. Their deaths almost wiped out all the full-blooded members of the Shinnecock tribe. All but one had families who were left destitute by this tragedy. They left nine widows and twenty-seven orphans. Those Indians who lost their lives were David, Franklin and Russell Bunn; Warren, George and William Cuffe; John and Lewis Walker; Robert Lee; and Oliver Kellis. Alphonse Elazer was the one Indian who came ashore in spite of the captain's threats not to pay him and have him blackballed from ever working on a ship again.

In an interview many years later, Captain Charlie Bennett said that as they stood on the beach they could hear the Indians singing "Nearer My God to Thee." The very religious Shinnecock were meeting death as courageously as they knew how.

There exists at the Southampton Historical Museum a letter to Hildreth's store from Mr. Theodore Roosevelt that included $217 to be distributed weekly to the bereaved Indian families. They also have a bill to the "Committee of Southampton" for the burial of the Indians.

THE WRECK OF THE SCHOONER *LOUISE H. RANDALL* AT SMITH'S POINT, LONG ISLAND

In the summer of 1891, the Randalls of Port Jefferson, Long Island, had just invested in a new schooner. They, along with other investors, had it built in East Boston, Massachusetts. The ship, the *Louise H. Randall*, was named after the captain's wife, who had joined him on his sea voyages.

The schooner's keel was laid in July of 1891. She was two hundred feet long with a forty-two-foot beam and a twenty-six-foot depth of hold. She was 1,500 tons and could carry 2,700 tons of cargo.

She was launched on April 28, 1892, with over four hundred invited guests in attendance. The ship was decked out with flags and a band played as the blocks were knocked away from under the keel. She slid majestically down the ways. By August of 1892 she had been fitted with a twenty-five-horsepower donkey engine for lifting sails and handling cargo.

The ship was intended to be home for Louise and Captain Randall. It had a living room finished in oak and mahogany. It had a piano made to order with matching wood. Like most furnishings, the piano was bolted to the deck. The stateroom was furnished with a brass bedstead. The schooner had the finest cabin of any vessel on the coast; she was equal to the appointments to many yachts.

In August 1892, she made her first trip to Philadelphia loaded with ice from Bangor, Maine. For fifteen months the crew made trips to and from Port Richmond, Philadelphia. On November 24, 1893, they left with 2,600 tons of hard coal for Boston.

Coastal shipping by this time was seeing an influx of European sailors. Aboard was First Mate Thomas Smith of Vineyard Haven, Massachusetts; Second Mate George S. Phillips of Chelsea, Massachusetts; steward John S. Adams of New York City; Engineer John Otto of Boston; and seamen Henry Theil of Germany, John Bgalrendund of Finland, George Leggett of Moriches, Long Island, and Emil Hammqvuist and Fredric Carlsen of Sweden.

As was the custom, they were towed down the Delaware River by a tug and sailed with the tide. Just as they approached Five Fathom Bank Lightship on the Jersey coast, the barometer began falling fast, promising a good southeast storm. Sailors of the day feared a sou'easter on the south side of Long Island. As the gale increased, the upper sails were taken in and furled. As it began to rain and the weather thickened, the sea grew rough. The cabin door was battened and the shutters closed, making ready for a bad blow.

The captain ordered Louise to stay below in her cabin. About ten o'clock on November 24, three seas came in quick succession, throwing the vessel on her beam-ends. This caused the cargo of coal to shift, throwing the ship out of trim. The ship failed to right and the port rail was under water. It washed everything off the decks, wiping them clean. The water burst through the ports and shutters, putting out the fire in the stove and the lamps and throwing the cabin into darkness.

After a panic attack, Louise forced her way out of the cabin, where the water was two feet deep and full of debris. Her husband tried to reassure her and told her that the ship was still manageable. He was heading for shallow water hoping to beach her, knowing the chances of a rescue were much better close to shore. Louise stood by the rail that was out of water, holding on for dear life. She was being drenched by every wave.

At 3:00 a.m. a sounding was taken with a lead line and it was found that they were in eleven fathoms of water. The starboard anchor was let go and one hundred fathoms of chain ran out before it parted. The captain figured that the ship would go ashore on the sandy beach between Fire Island and Shinnecock. As they grew near to the beach the captain shouted, "To the rigging for your lives!" Louise lost her blanket in the mad dash into the rigging. After a while the captain instructed everyone to go forward to the fore rigging when there was a lull. All but two made the mad dash. The ship sank into the sand of the outer bar about a half mile from the beach.

At dawn, they were able to see the lifesaving crews on the beach attempting to rescue them. The ship was seven hundred yards from shore, farther than the Lyle gun's normal range. The wind-driven rain was howling out of the southeast. The breakers were too high to launch a surfboat. After several hours, the captain told his crew to leave the shrouds for the comparative safety of the crosstrees. There were two crosstrees to each mast, about a hundred feet up, with about two feet between them. They were only four inches wide.

The captain had some lines cut loose by a seaman on the crosstrees and passed the line under the arms of Louise, his frightened wife. In this fashion, Louise was lifted up to the perch and lashed fast to the mast. Eventually there were nine people on the narrow pieces of wood. There were five on one side and four on the other, all lashed fast. The ship's deck had disappeared beneath the waves. They watched as the crews ashore attempted to shoot lines aboard with the Lyle gun and the experimental Cunningham rocket that they had.

Ashore, Captain Jack Penney of the Smith Point Station had called in crews from seven stations, from Westhampton to Blue Point. The morning found debris from the disintegrating pieces of the ship strewn along the beach. The 2,600-pound boiler from the donkey engine had been hurled upon the beach. Each crew in turn tried its hand at putting a line aboard, but to no avail. Night was approaching; the rain had stopped but the wind continued unabated. The men and the one woman could be seen plainly from shore. Those in the rigging had not eaten or drank anything in twenty-four hours. The masts stayed upright, probably held in part by the load of coal in the hold. When the lifesavers' efforts failed, they telephoned New York for aid from the Lifesaving Benevolent Association.

The lifesaving crews had given up all hope of a rescue from the shore until the seas calmed a bit. Great fires were built on the beach so that the shipwrecked would know that there were still crews waiting to save them.

Sometime after midnight, Captain Randall saw from his perch the lights of a steamer and saw them launch a small boat, which turned back. The wrecking steamer was the *I.J. Merritt*, which had been dispatched from Stapleton, Staten Island, to effect a rescue from seaward.

Their "cargo surfboat" had caught a large wave, which smashed it against the steamer, damaging it. The same wave ripped the cabin door from the ship's galley. The boat was repaired with canvas and battens and launched again with eight oarsmen and one man on the steering oar. They were unable to row against the wind, so the steamer towed them into a position where they could blow down on the stricken schooner. They anchored in seven fathoms of water and worked the surfboat to within three hundred feet of the wreck's stern. They returned to the steamer and waited for morning. This time they were able to drop a grapple to hold them off from the ship and ease their way in. They took the two men from the main rigging and worked the boat up to the fore rigging, where they removed the remainder of the men and Louise. Those rescued were immediately furnished with blankets and water.

Meanwhile, Captain Penney had managed to launch the surfboat. Soon after launching, the boat was damaged by a large wave. Two of the men had to bail as the surfboat pulled for the steamer. Penney knew that they would not be able to make it back to shore, so he headed for the steamer. The sinking surfboat was pulled aboard the steamer.

Breakfast was served to the rescued aboard the *I.J. Merritt*, but they were unable to eat. The ship left for New York with both rescued crews aboard. By this time they had been thirty-eight hours without food or drink.

Captain Penney had to borrow money from a friend in New York in order to pay for passage for himself and his crew to get back to Mastic. The surfboat was repaired and came back on a Long Island Railroad flatcar.

The wreck was well attended. One of those attending was Horace Raynor, a retired sailor and part-time scribe for the *Brooklyn Eagle*. He had been duck hunting on nearby Pattersquash Island. He wanted to get the story in but needed the name of the vessel. He and his brother, who had accompanied him, searched through the debris on the beach for something with the ship's name. They were successful and they wrote the name on a barrel stave for Captain Penney, and then left for the telegraph office at the Mastic Railroad Station, asking him to give them a head start before revealing the name to the others.

Captain Penney had ordered the families of the surfmen to stay off the beach because of the severity of the storm. They would normally act as a cheering section and a source of hot food and drink. Captain Penney's wife, Ella May Ketcham, and eleven-year-old daughter Ethel lived at the station. Later on, little Ethel found the piano stool from the ship. It now resides at the Moriches Bay Historic Society's museum in Center Moriches.

Captain and Mrs. Penney and the Randalls later became friends. After this misadventure the Randalls retired to the island of Martha's Vineyard, where they spent the rest of their lives.

Another eyewitness to the event was Dr. George S. King, then a fifteen-year-old schoolboy who played hooky from Patchogue High School along with a buddy. They took a fourteen-foot sailboat from East Patchogue to Smith Point, about fifteen miles diagonally across Bellport Bay, with a gale blowing, with spray freezing on the rigging and no visibility. They were drenched to the skin in spite of heavy clothing, oilskins and rubber boots. All this made no difference; there was a great wreck to see and they just had to be there.

They landed on the beach about six miles west of the action, which was the best they could do with headwinds. The snow and ice on the beach made it impossible for them to walk, so they returned to the bay and waded through the shoal water, finally reaching Smith Point.

They, along with other bystanders, helped the lifesavers move the Lyle gun and apparatus carts around on the beach. After the rescue, most of them returned to the mainland at Smith's Point via small rowboats. King and his friend had been offered shelter at the Bellport Station by Captain William Kraemer, whom they often visited during better weather. After walking several miles on the frozen beach, they borrowed blankets from the lifesaving crew and went to sleep in the unheated boathouse for the second time.

Their trip home across Bellport Bay was an adventure in itself. They found their boat where they had left it, behind Fiddleton Flats, encrusted with snow. The wind was still blowing a gale, but this time it was behind them. They took off, not realizing that the bay was full of "lumps and floes of ice." Their boat became unmanageable and they took down what little sail they had up, sailing with a bare mast. The ice made them fashion a fender of rolled-up sail, which they fastened around the bow. Some of it was used like a fender to soften the blows. With one steering and the other fending off chunks of ice, they made their way back across the bay.

Dr. King stated many years later, "Those four or five hours of hard work with our little cockleshell was one of the most dangerous and foolhardy trips I have undertaken. We finally arrived in East Patchogue, ran the boat up East Creek and tied her to the bank. When we got home we assured our families that at no time had we been in danger but had been nice and warm the whole trip."

After the rescue, the ship went gradually to pieces, leaving only the bowsprit sticking out of the water. Beachcombers picked up coal that washed ashore all winter and many local homes were heated with it.

When the rescued crew members arrived in New York they were met by the other owners of the schooner and brought to the Presbyterian Hospital at East Seventieth Street. Louise was treated for a badly mangled foot and general exposure.

THE COAL SCHOONER *AUGUSTUS HUNT* WRECKED AT QUOGUE

Sea disasters along Long Island's coastline became well known by the telling and retelling of these events. Such was the case with the coal schooner *Augustus Hunt*. On January 22, 1904, the four-masted schooner from Norfolk, Virginia, with 1,750 tons of bituminous coal aboard for Boston, plowed hard into the bar about one and a half miles west of the Quogue Lifesaving Station opposite the halfway house. There was a moderate gale blowing, a heavy sea and thick fog.

The mate had reported a light ahead shortly before stranding. It was taken to be another ship. The moment the ship hit, seas instantly swept her deck from stern to stem, breaking halfway up the spars. All aboard took to the rigging immediately. The light they had seen was the Shinnecock lighthouse. The fog was so thick that the sailors could not see land and the lifesavers could not see the ship. The time of the stranding was 11:45 p.m. At midnight, surfman Levi Crasper left the Quogue station for the west patrol. About half an hour later, he thought he could discern a dark spot in the fog offshore. He watched for a while and, seeing nothing, he continued along the beach until he met surfman Herman Bishop from the Potunk (Westhampton) station. Together they went back to the spot. After watching closely, they both concluded that there was a vessel on the bar. Crasper burnt his Coston flare, which according to the survivors they saw briefly, but they had no way of signaling back. Both surfmen dashed back to their respective stations to report the event. By 2:00 a.m. the crews from Quogue and Potunk were on scene. The fog had lifted enough that a ship was barely discernible. The crews set to work digging through the frozen sand to set the sand anchor and set up the breeches buoy apparatus. The Lyle gun was fired at the vague target in the fog. No one took up the line on the ship's end, so every time they got a break in the fog another line was fired.

Keeper Charles A. Carter and his crew from Tiana station arrived at 3:00 a.m., having been alerted by telephone. Keeper Charles Hermann, who was in charge, decided to try the boat in spite of the fact that everyone was of the opinion that it could not be done. By this time there were numbers of local people on the beach, many of them knowledgeable surf boatmen. There was white water as far as they could see in the direction of the wreck. After thirty minutes of trying to launch, the effort was abandoned.

At 9:00 a.m., there was a break in the fog and the outline of the schooner could be seen for a few minutes. The surfboat was again launched, but had not made it more than twenty feet when it turned over, spilling the men into the icy water. Both men and boat came rolling in on the breakers.

For a mile along the shore, the beach and the surf were filled with wreckage from the doomed ship. Between six and seven in the morning the cries of the men could be heard weakly. About that time a loud crash was heard above the noise of the surf. The survivors later stated three of the masts came down. About ten minutes later the fourth mast crashed into the sea, ending the lives of seven of the sailors. The remaining three had taken refuge on the jib boom. As the boom began to break, the three crawled back to the forecastle and two of them jumped off onto some floating wreckage near the remains of the ship. The third man just disappeared. He either drowned or was killed in the seething mass of wreckage; his shipmates did not witness his demise.

Second mate George Eberts and seaman Carl Sommers were the two still alive. They had jumped to a large piece of the deck, which was still fast to the remains of the vessel and was smashing into the vessel with every wave. It finally broke loose and started to float toward shore. As it got to within two hundred yards of shore, the two could be seen clinging to some upright pieces about thirty feet apart. This was the first time the lifesavers got a good look at their desperate situation, the fog being so thick that they never actually saw the ship, according to Halsey in a letter written many years later.

The surfmen again fired their Lyle gun and managed to get a line across the floating piece of wreckage. The second shot was close enough to one man that he was able to pull it toward himself with his foot. He quickly made it fast to the wreckage, which was continually awash. As soon as the surfmen on shore pulled the line taut, the seaman threw one arm over the line and with it tucked into his armpit started to make his way toward shore and safety over the top of the floating debris. He had made his way about ten yards toward shore when a large wave dislodged him from the line. At that moment, surfman William Halsey Jr. tied a heaving line around his waist, rushed into the breakers and clambered onto the floating wreckage. He was in immediate danger of being crushed, but managed to work his way to the exhausted man and drag him toward the beach, where a human chain of lifesavers grabbed them both and pulled them ashore. Eberts was quickly placed in a bystander's wagon and taken to the station for first aid.

As the surfmen were about to shoot another line closer to the second man, he managed to crawl over to the side where the line was without being washed overboard. He began his perilous trip over the wreckage on the line with surf breaking over him. He soon stopped moving, as the icy water started to take its toll and his arms would no longer function. At that moment surfman Frank Warner jumped into the water and proceeded toward the helpless man. He was able to drag the man back to the surf line where Winfield Jessup, a local citizen, and Keeper Gildersleeve waded in and dragged both men to safety. Gildersleeve was knocked down by the waves in the process.

Witnesses stated that the flesh of the rescued man, Carl Sommers, had started to turn blue. He was quickly placed in the wagon under the care of another local citizen, Mr. Erastus F. Post, and was taken to Dr. Brundage of Westhampton Beach for medical treatment. A total of two lives were saved and eight were lost in this wreck.

After the weather improved, the coroner, Dr. John Nugent, and his associate Mr. George Winters arrived to take charge of the remains. They were standing on a heavy piece of wreckage at low tide that had a body caught under it. The coroner directed surfman Halsey to take an axe and cut the leg off so they could remove the body. This was done and the body was removed in a piece of canvas not much bigger than a bath towel. "I do not believe there was a bone left unbroken in the body," stated Mr. Winters.

Lieutenant DeOtte of the U.S. Revenue Marines soon arrived to conduct an inquiry into the eight deaths, as was customary.

The scene of the wreck was visited daily by a large number of sightseers, all of whom carried away a piece of the wreckage for a souvenir.

The wheel from the *Augustus Hunt* was at the Yardarm Club at Westhampton Beach in 1950. The anchor was at the gateway belonging to a Mr. Taylor of Quogue, according to Mr. Winters, in a letter to Harry B. Squires years later.

Captain Robert Blair, the real captain, had been sick, so the first mate sailed as acting captain of "Jumbo," as the *Hunt* was known. Acting as agent for the company, he arrived and sold most of the wreckage to Silas Tuttle for fifteen dollars.

The survivors said that no soundings were taken and the last known position was at the Five Fathom Bank Lightship off South Jersey, which helps explain how the ship plowed directly into the beach.

On June 4, 1904, at an annual dinner and meeting of the Long Island Surfmen at Roe's Hotel in Patchogue, both Halsey and Warner were presented with the service's highest honor, the gold lifesaving medal. Raynor and Latham of the Blue Point Station were similarly rewarded for their similar rescue from the wreck of the *Benjamin C. Cromwel* at Bellport. Halsey's gold medal was still in the possession of the family in 1996.

William Fanning Halsey Jr. retired July 1, 1931, as a warrant boatswain (L), USCG, after being in charge of the Quogue Station for many years. He had joined in 1901. He worked summers at the bathing beach next door to the station and had won medals in swimming contests.

By 1930, Frank Warner had become a warrant boatswain and was in charge of the Ditch Plains Coast Guard Station four miles west of Montauk. Four days' worth of fog that November resulted in three ships on the rocks near the station: a collier, a steam trawler and a rumrunner. With small boat and breeches buoy, all crews were rescued and 1,100 cases of liquor were confiscated. That time there were photographers and movies cameramen to record the events. Frank Daniel Warner retired in 1934.

1907: *WILLIAM C. CARNEGIE*, FIVE-MASTED COAL SCHOONER, AGROUND AT MORICHES IN A NORTHEAST GALE

There was money to be made moving large amounts of coal from the late 1800s through the early 1900s. Owners of schooners were loading coal at Philadelphia and Virginia ports, and transporting it to New England ports. This growth industry spawned the J.S. Winslow Company, which had schooners built for the express purpose of carrying coal. It was this fleet that helped keep the lifesavers along Long Island's south shore employed. The industrial Northeast was always hungry for coal, so the schooners sailed in bad weather as well as good. The inevitable result was more shipwrecks along Long Island's south shore.

Fire, the scourge of coal-laden ships on long offshore voyages, struck at very infrequent intervals among the coastal colliers. They were at sea too short a time for spontaneous combustion to develop. But fire did break out aboard the vessel *Charles L. Davenport*, out of Philadelphia for Bangor, Maine, in July of 1900. A salvage tug was called and was able to put out the fire and tow the ship in for repair.

On May 1, 1909, at 2:50 a.m., the *William C. Carnegie*, a five-masted coal carrier, hit the bar about six hundred yards off the beach, just a short ways from the Moriches Station. She was loaded with 4,400 tons of bituminous coal. There was a northeaster blowing and Captain Reed was unable to take a fix on the stars. This was scarcely six weeks after the *Miles M. Merry*, owned by the same company, had beached at almost the same spot. Two years before, the *Merry* had been hauled off from the same spot by the Merritt-Chapman Wrecking Company.

By 3:45 a.m., lifesavers from Moriches, Potunk and Forge River were firing the Lyle gun to put a line aboard, but she was out of range. By dawn the ship was starting to break up. Captain "Rose" Gordon and Captain Isaac Gildersleeve attempted to launch a surfboat, but waves twenty feet high threw them out of the boat and they, along with the overturned boat, washed up on the beach. It was decided to call for the U.S. revenue cutter *Mohawk* to come to the crew's rescue. Using the beach telephone system, Captain Gordon called the navy wireless station near the Fire Island Lighthouse to signal the *Mohawk* to come as fast as possible.

When the ship started to break up, the captain and the eleven-man crew got into their small yawl and left. The lifesavers signaled them, probably by semaphore, not to try to land. The heavy seas would have dumped them into the surf. The lifesavers trained weekly to land on the beach in the surf, which can be tricky and dangerous. The men in the yawl waited around all day near their disintegrating ship with cold ocean spray blowing over them, keeping them wet and cold. As evening approached, the *Mohawk* arrived. To complicate matters, it had turned foggy. Guided by fires lit by the lifesavers on the beach, a search was made that was eventually successful. Once the rescued crew of the *Carnegie* was safely onboard the revenue cutter, it took off for New York.

The *Carnegie* was blown broadside to the beach, where she continued to break up. Pieces of cabin furniture, torn sails and rigging were strewn along the beach. It was the lifesavers job to collect and hold such cargo and material for the owners to reclaim. The ship was given up as a complete loss. She had been built at a cost of $125,000 nine years earlier and had a value of about $70,000 before the accident. The cargo of coal was valued at $12,000 and was covered by insurance.

The J.S. Winslow Company of Portland, Maine, owned both the *Miles M. Merry* and the *William C. Carnegie*. According to Captain Lou Pearsall, the company gave the remains of the ship to Captain Gordon and his crew. They were able to salvage the rigging and all of the sails. The masts and spars were smashed to pieces by the furious seas that battered the stranded vessel.

The five-masted ship Carnegie had been built in Bath, Maine, by Percy and Small at what is today the site of the Maine Maritime Museum. She was the first Percy and Small vessel to incorporate steel strapping for hull reinforcement. Coal was a tough cargo on the ship, as it was stored loose. The coal had to be constantly shoveled as the ship was loaded to trim the weight.

The launch was to be on August 11, 1900. There were ten thousand people assembled to watch the launching in the ninety-four-degree heat of the day. The launching was timed to coincide with Bath's celebration of "Old Home Week."

The excessive heat took its toll, dissipating the grease used to lubricate the ship's ways and incapacitating Miss Grace Winslow, who was scheduled to launch the vessel. The master builder, Willard Hodgkins, was unable to get the ship to budge. It was August 13 before the ship finally was launched. Hodgkins was disgraced and never built another ship for Percy and Small. Miles Merry, no doubt the person for whom the *Miles M. Merry* was named, oversaw the delayed launching.

The *Carnegie* was the first of the great schooners to be equipped with two stockless anchors. The stockless anchor was patented by Baldt, the manufacturer, in 1897, with a patent modification in 1901.

The wreck of the *Carnegie* made several appearances in the surf line on the beach near what is now Westhampton Dunes. In 1959, the ribs of an old ship became visible after a northeast storm, along with a large anchor. Several days later it again appeared underneath the shifting sands. Two years later, in December of 1961, James Doyle of the Westhampton Beach Police told Sam Cross, a local historian and engineer in Westhampton Beach, that he had spotted the wreck again. Cross in turn notified the Suffolk County Public Works Department. In 1967, the anchor, along with a smaller one, was retrieved from the sand and both were stored in the Suffolk County Facility at Yaphank.

In the early 1980s, one anchor was removed to the Westhampton Beach Village Green on Mill Road and Main Street, just west of the post office. It was displayed there until the 1990s, when it was moved to its present resting place in the Westhampton Beach Municipal Marina.

1907: PASSENGER STEAMER *LARCHMONT* COLLIDES WITH SCHOONER

The late 1800s and early 1900s found luxury side wheel–propelled steamers plying Long Island Sound waters, furnishing transportation from the New York area to Providence, Rhode Island, and Boston. These ships were eventually replaced with a passenger railroad line. The *Larchmont* and the *Tremont* were owned by the New York, New Haven & Hartford Railroad under the name of the Joy Line. These were wooden hulled boats, built in the 1880s in Bath, Maine. The *Larchmont* was a side-wheel, single-deck, two-masted steamer.

The *Larchmont* sailed from Providence at 7:00 p.m. February 11, 1907. There were gale-force winds and the temperature was hovering around zero degrees. Captain McVey said that they passed Point Judith at about 9:30 p.m. on a southwesterly course. The spray was being carried over the vessel by the wind and freezing as it hit, coating everything with ice.

Traveling in a northeasterly direction, from New Jersey to Boston, with a load of soft coal was the three-masted schooner *Harry P. Knowlton*. She was commanded by Captain Frank T. Haley and was carrying a crew of seven. She had been stuck in the ice floes in Long Island Sound, and upon breaking free she hoisted all available canvas and was making up for lost time. The night was clear and she was steering for the Point Judith Light, putting her on a reciprocal course to the *Larchmont*.

The weather was clear, but the wind-driven spray freezing on both vessels must have made visibility a problem. When the *Knowlton* first spotted the *Larchmont* on a collision course, Captain Haley expected them to veer off, giving the right of way to the sailing vessel. He was afraid if he changed course the other ship might do the same, thus causing a collision. In the end, both ships held to their respective courses, resulting in the 317-ton schooner *Knowlton* ramming the 1,605-ton *Larchmont* on the forward port quarter. The two vessels collided at around 10:45 p.m. about two and three quarter miles south-southeast of the Watch Hill Light, about eleven miles from the north end of Block Island.

According to Captain Haley, he was sounding the *Knowlton*'s foghorn to attract attention. It would appear that Captain McVey never saw the schooner until it was too late. Their stories varied after the disaster.

The momentum of the *Larchmont* carried her forward, out of sight of the *Knowlton*, which was trying to signal her own distress. The *Knowlton* was leaking badly, so the captain turned the vessel northward toward the nearest land to beach her. While she was about a mile and a half off the beach at Quonochontaug, Rhode Island, near the lifesaving station, the captain and crew took to their small boat and rowed for shore. Both vessels were spotted by the lifesaver on beach patrol. He assisted the men ashore. The ship came ashore and became a total loss. The men were taken to the station, where they were cared for for three days. The men of the *Knowlton* didn't realize the seriousness of the disaster because they were out of sight of the *Larchmont* before the damage was known. The full extent of the disaster was not known until Captain McVey made it to shore and reported to the keeper at the lifesaving station.

Following the collision, the *Larchmont* began taking on large amounts of water through the gaping hole in her side. The steam pipe burst, throwing live steam about, and the lights went out almost immediately.

Many of those aboard had already retired and were in their bedclothes. In the ensuing pandemonium, many reached the deck thinly clad; others were drowned in their beds. In the general confusion, the crew was attempting to lower the eight lifeboats and four rafts. The task was made more difficult by frozen hands refusing to work frozen lines. The collision broke the communication line between the bridge and the engine room so the captain had no idea what was going on below deck. When the captain took to his boat, the ship was so low in the water it was only necessary to cast off the lines.

The *Larchmont* sank in less than fifteen minutes. People were clinging to boats and rafts. The forty-five-mile-an-hour wind and the freezing spray ended the lives of most of the passengers and crew. There were about thirty in the crew and around one hundred passengers. No one seemed to know the exact count. The purser had left the list in the safe aboard.

The wind carried the survivors and the dead toward the Sandy Point Light on the north end of Block Island. The Sandy Point Life-Saving Station was nearby.

A nearly frozen boy who had drifted ashore in a boat with others made it to the lighthouse. The keeper called the lifesaving station, which dispatched surfmen to look for a ship ashore. They administered first aid to the boy, who told them of the disaster and the others possibly on the beach.

Next, they found lifeboat number 8 washed up with surf breaking into it. They found one man encased in ice. They managed to remove him and carry him to the lighthouse. The local doctor was called to the shipwrecked persons. The lifesavers found others ashore struggling to reach the station.

The keeper contacted some local people to search the beach for survivors. The news of the disaster spread quickly through the small community, and shortly after daylight nearly every islander was down on the beaches braving the cold and awaiting the opportunity to assist the victims. Nearly every survivor was in such bad shape that the rescuers wept over them. Their feet were frozen and they had to be carried. They were in such a dazed condition that they hardly recognized that they had been rescued. Today, we know the condition as hypothermia.

The survivors who were being cared for at the lifesaving station were soon taken in by the islanders and made comfortable, the station being too small to handle so many disabled. It wasn't until Captain McVey came ashore that the lifesavers learned the extent of the disaster. Captain McVey called the keeper at the New Shoreham

Station on the south end of Block Island. He responded with men, blankets and clothing. Usable clothing and blankets were furnished to stations by the volunteer effort of the Women's National Relief Association. Without this invaluable assistance, the lifesavers would have been hard-pressed to help the shipwrecked sailors.

Later on toward noon, a man with a team of oxen and a wagon was enlisted to drive along the beach and pick up the bodies that the lifesavers had pulled above the surf line. Boat number 6 was found about the same time. It contained one man still alive and nine frozen bodies, including one man who had cut his own throat because he couldn't stand the intense cold. For two days six surfmen patrolled the beach continuously, looking for more survivors or more bodies.

On February 12, the New Shoreham crew returned to their station, having received word that survivors were arriving at Old Harbor aboard fishing schooners. Some of the rafts had missed the island and were picked up by these ships. The *Elsie* arrived with eight survivors and seven dead. The schooner *Clara E.* came in with thirteen bodies. Another thirteen had arrived on other small fishing schooners. The Joy Steamship Company sent the steamer *Kentucky* to carry the dead and the survivors back to Providence. As more bodies accumulated, they were shipped to Providence aboard the Joy Line's tug *Roger Williams*.

Of the twenty persons who made landfall alive, three did not survive the exposure to the elements that night. The bitter cold was such that in the same newspaper there was a story of a man in New York found frozen to a lamppost. A policeman used his night stick to pry him loose. In doing so, the man lost the skin from the palms of his hands.

In the moments leading up to the collision of the *Larchmont* and the *Knowlton*, neither vessel sent up a distress signal. Had they done so, there was a good chance one of the beach patrols would have spotted them, as the night was clear and they were less than three miles from land.

The newspapers featured stories about the wreck and the actions of the captain. A boy claimed that the captain was the first to leave. The captain claimed that he was attempting to circle the ship to see what was happening on the starboard side, which he was unable to see. A young lady claimed that she was prevented from entering the captain's lifeboat.

The *Larchmont* was a hard luck ship. The 252-foot wooden ship was built in Bath, Maine, in 1885. In her early days, she was in a collision in Boston Harbor and sank. In 1902, she was afire on Long Island Sound. The two hundred passengers were panic-stricken, but the crew got the flames under control and she made port safely. Two years later, she ran down the lumber-laden schooner *D.T. Melanson* off Stratford, and the same year she was grounded twice, once in Narragansett Bay and once off Prudence Island. Early in 1905, a fire started onboard when she was off North Brother Island due to faulty insulation near her boilers. This was the location of the *General Slocum* fiery disaster the year before.

Today the wreck is marked on chart number 13205 south of Watch Hill Point and east of the Mo (A) whistle buoy. It was a headline story in the *New York Times* for several days. Today it is a dive site and can be found on the Internet.

THE ROYAL MAIL SHIP *REPUBLIC* SANK AFTER COLLISION OFF NANTUCKET

On the morning of January 23, 1909, the RMS *Republic* had left New York Harbor and was bound for the Mediterranean with 742 vacationing passengers and crew. What the contents of her hold contained is still a mystery.

The White Star ship was built for the carriage trade with onboard opulence and comfort, rather than speed. On the six-day crossing, passengers would spend their time dining in style and drinking the best wines, dancing to the music of fine orchestras and being served by an attentive staff of servants. She was a cruise ship intending to ply the sunny Mediterranean Sea for two months.

Passengers could enjoy something new aboard ships. A newspaper was printed daily aboard with news and stock reports copied by the ship's wireless operator. The wireless aboard was thought of as a luxury rather than a safety device.

In the hours before dawn on that January morning, the ship encountered a fog bank. Captain Inman Sealby ordered a small reduction in the speed. He was in open sea in the Nantucket traffic lane south of Nantucket Island. The ship was sounding the fog signal in accordance with International Rules of the Road. At about 5:30 a.m., an answering fog signal was heard off the port bow. The captain immediately ordered full astern and the helm to hard a-port, while signaling his intention with his foghorn. Out of the fog appeared the bow of a ship. The oncoming ship hit *Republic* amidships, killing three passengers as they slept. The ships soon drifted apart and out of sight in the fog. Water was pouring into the engine and boiler rooms, killing the lights, and soon the ship was listing.

The crash awakened the young Marconi wireless operator Jack Binns, who discovered his cabin was in shambles. The wireless shack had its roof torn away by the impact. As there was no power, he hooked up the emergency batteries and sent out a distress call. He sent the newly agreed upon Marconi Company signal "CQD." It was the first use of this abbreviation in such a large, life-threatening situation. CQ is a general call to all listening and the D stood for distress. By the time of the *Titanic* sinking in 1912, this code had been replaced by the new international distress signal dubbed "SOS" because it resembled the Morse characters; however, the dots and dashes are run together, making one character.

Jack Irwin, the operator on duty at the Marconi station on nearby Nantucket, picked up the distress signal and relayed it so the world was soon informed. The U.S. Revenue Cutter Service, forerunner of the U.S. Coast Guard, dispatched two cutters, *Seneca* from New York City and *Gresham* from Boston, to the scene. The *Baltic*, *LaLorraine*, salvage tug *City of Everett* and the revenue cutter *Acushnet* from Woods Hole, upon hearing the distress call, all rushed toward the location of the collision.

This was the first demonstration of the Marconi's wireless ability to aid victims of disasters at sea. It would be another three years before the United States would require passenger ships to carry wireless. It is interesting to note that the other operator at Nantucket was a recent trainee of Marconi's named David Sarnoff, who went on to become the president of the Radio Corporation of America (RCA), which later absorbed the American Marconi company.

Meanwhile, the Italian ship *Florida* had suffered her bow pushed in and three crewmen killed in the collision. Fortunately the *Florida* wasn't leaking, as the damage was above the waterline. She was on her way from Italy with 900 hundred Italian immigrants. As a result of the earthquake on December 28, 1908, in Messina, Italy, the Italian government arranged steamship transportation for many of the traumatized survivors to go to America in steerage, whether they wanted to or not. There were more than 200,000 dead and countless others left homeless. The ship's captain was only twenty-eight years old, but he performed admirably in the circumstance in which he found himself.

The *Florida* returned to the scene of the accident and was able to take aboard all of the *Republic*'s passengers and most of the crew. This was not an easy task at sea for the smaller, damaged *Florida.*

Meanwhile Jack Binns, the *Republic*'s wireless operator, kept in communication with the White Star Liner *Baltic.* By noon the next day, the *Baltic* was about ten miles from the disaster scene. The fog remained heavy so the ship was moving very slowly with extra lookouts on duty. It was arranged by wireless for the ships to signal via small signaling bombs. The ships' chronometers were synchronized via wireless and their crews listened attentively for the noise. Nothing was heard until they were down to their last bomb. The eight left on the *Republic* formed a circle looking out and listening intently. Two thought they heard a faint noise so the course was sent to the *Baltic*, and in about fifteen minutes their foghorn was heard. By that time Jack Binns had been at his post at the wireless with no food and no heat, day and night, until he was ordered off the sinking ship by the captain shortly before its final plunge.

The French government gave Jack Binns a medal for his heroism as wireless operator. In 1912 he was slated for a post on the *Titanic*, but love intervened to save him. He had just gotten married and did not wish to leave his new wife to go to sea again.

The White Star Liner *Baltic* finally arrived and the passengers were again transferred, this time to the *Baltic*, as the *Florida* had lost thirty feet of bow accordioned into the ship and was severely overloaded with all the people aboard. The women and children were transferred first, then the rest of the first-class passengers and finally all of *Florida*'s passengers. A riot almost ensued because the Italian steerage passengers felt they were being considered last. The transfer at sea of so many people took eight hours. This left the *Florida* to limp into port for repairs while the *Baltic* brought the passengers to New York, minus their jewels and luggage.

Most of the *Republic*'s crew, as well as the passengers, had been put on the *Baltic*. Captain Sealby and eight others remained with the sinking "unsinkable" ship along with the wireless operator.

Jack Binns reported in an interview years later,

> *When daylight broke the next morning, it revealed one of the greatest concourses of ships ever seen on the seas. Everywhere, as far as the eye could see were ships. Every liner and every cargo ship equipped with wireless that happened to be within a 300 mile radius of the disaster, overhearing the exchange of messages between the* Baltic *and* Republic *had gathered around and stood by ready to be of whatever assistance they could. It was a fine testimonial to the value of wireless.*

The 15,000-ton, 570-foot *Republic*, with a 70-foot beam, was taken in tow by the two revenue cutters, *Seneca* and *Gresham*, bound for the shallow water around Nantucket. They tried to tow at two knots. The Anchor liner *Furnessia* had tied up to the stern to act as a rudder for the disabled ship. At about 8:00 p.m., with their searchlights on the tow, it was determined that the giant ship was rapidly sinking!

The tow started at 10:00 a.m. Sunday morning and continued until 7:00 p.m. Sunday night. No actual progress was being made, as the strong current they were bucking was the same speed as their forward motion, so all four ships stood virtually still.

The *Furnessia* cast off her line as the stern of the *Republic* was under water, flooding the wireless room. At this time the captain ordered the rest of the crew off, save one volunteer to stay with him. The rest departed in the captain's gig.

> *At this time the* Republic *was attached to the* Gresham *by a steel hawser. As soon as we put off in the Captain's gig we pulled over to the* Gresham, *told the Captain of that ship the condition of the* Republic, *and asked him to pay out a nine-inch rope hawser and stand by, ready to cut the hawser as soon as he got a signal from the bridge of the* Republic *that the ship was about to go under. It had been previously agreed that Captain Sealby was to flash a blue Coston light when the moment did arrive.*
>
> *This, the Captain of the* Gresham *did. He stationed a man with an ax over the hawser, with instructions to cut it the moment he saw*

the blue light. We stayed off in the lifeboat waiting for developments and holding ourselves ready to go to the rescue of Sealby and Williams the moment the ship went down.

Fortunately there were four or five other ships in the vicinity watching the proceedings. Each one played his searchlight on the Republic. *By the aid of many searchlights, the two lone figures could be seen pacing to and fro on the up tilted bridge. Then came the signal of the blue light. Then we saw one of the men jump on to the rat-lines of the foremast, climb up to the top of the mast and wait. The other man ran forward, jumped up on the rail, and taking one last long look at the little cabin on the bridge, turned and dove 40 feet into the sea. For one minute more the bow of the* Republic *trembled above the waves and then sank.*

We rowed to the spot where it went down. The light of each observing ship was trained upon the spot. Fortunately a quiet sea was running at the time, but even so it was most difficult to see very far from the open boat as the lights, intercepted by the crests of the waves, threw darkened shadows over most of the surrounding water.

For 20 minutes we rowed around, earnestly but yet aimlessly, for we did not know where to go. On all sides, we saw glaring searchlights, but nowhere could we discern any sign of life in the sea. I don't think any more sorrowful moment ever came to the lives of the men in the open boat, not to mention those on the nearby ships, for Captain Sealby and Second Officer Williams had nobly upheld the tradition of the sea. But the length of time did not diminish our hopes.

Suddenly, to our right, from out of the murky blackness of the waters of the sea, a revolver shot rang out. We pulled over in that direction immediately, and found Captain Sealby hanging on to a floating crate, so nearly exhausted that he had just sufficient strength to pull the trigger of his revolver. "Williams over there," he said, "get him." But we pulled the Captain in and sure enough we found Williams too, clinging to a hatch cover that had floated off the Republic *as she went down.*

At the time of this interview in the April 1924 issue of *Radio Broadcast*, Binns was working as the radio editor of the *New York Tribune*. This may explain the rather vivid account that he gave of the event fifteen years afterward.

Why did the captain wait for the last possible moment to abandon his ship? Perhaps it had to do with the chance a salver might have been able to save and claim the ship and cargo.

The sinking took place in forty fathoms, nine nautical miles west-southwest of the Nantucket lightship. The exact positions given by the two revenue cutters in their reports was about eight miles apart. In 1981, the wreck was located about halfway in between the two positions. The sunken remains were found six miles from the charted location.

At this point in the story the facts have been told; now begins the conjecture. Captain Sealby surrendered his captain's license, as was the custom after a wreck. It was to be reinstated after a court of inquiry had determined that he was blameless. However, the required board of inquiry was never held, leaving the captain without a job. He went back to school and took up maritime law, which he practiced in San Francisco until World War I, when he went back to sea serving as a transport captain with the Merchant Marine.

It is believed that the ship was carrying a secret cargo of gold destined for France, to be loaned to Czarist Russia to pay for the war with Japan that they were engaged in at the time. The amount was said to be fifteen tons of gold bars and 3 million 1909 dollars in $20 gold pieces in mint condition. In addition, there was a large sum of money destined for relief of the victims of an earthquake in Italy. There was also a $265,000 payroll aboard for the U.S. Navy fleet that was in the Mediterranean on a goodwill tour promoted by President Teddy Roosevelt.

All government records of the cargo seem to be missing. Captain Martin Bayerle formed a dive corporation to salvage the gold and silver from the ship. It is believed that there may be as much as $15 billion aboard! The loss of so much gold in 1909 could have caused a panic in the world markets and may have been hushed up because of this.

1919: THE GROUNDING OF THE STEAMSHIP *NORTHERN PACIFIC* AT FIRE ISLAND

One of the strangest shipwrecks to take place on Long Island's south shore happened at 2:30 a.m. January 1, 1919, New Year's Day. The official weather entry in the Fire Island Coast Guard log at 4:00

a.m. stated that the wind was southwest, wind speed around nine knots, barometer 30.02, rain and the temperature was fifty degrees. The *Northern Pacific* was making twenty knots on a course of 276 degrees true, as reported by the ship's navigator. The problem was that he thought he was ten miles farther south than he actually was. The man on watch failed to see the Fire Island Light until shortly before the grounding. He reported a light half point on the port bow, but apparently he did not recognize it as the Fire Island Light. The navigator stated at the official inquiry that the light was visible twenty-seven miles from the bridge. The captain and navigator were notified, but the grounding occurred as they were making their way to the bridge. They had expected to pass five and a half miles south of the Fire Island Lightship, or fifteen miles south of the lighthouse, at 3:00 a.m. Instead, the ship bounced over a couple of bars and came to rest about three hundred yards off the beach, about one and a half miles east of the Fire Island Lighthouse in front of a few summer shacks in a placed called Lonelyville.

The *Northern Pacific* was a luxury liner built by the Northern Pacific Railroad for runs between Seattle, San Francisco and Honolulu at a cost of $2.5 million. She was being used to transport wounded soldiers and sailors from France back to the United States under the command of the U.S. Navy. Strictly speaking, she was not a hospital ship, but a troop transport. Her wartime camouflage paint is visible in the photographs.

Her course was supposed to take her down a corridor that had been swept by minesweepers. This was the area where the USS *San Diego* had been sunk by a German mine six months earlier. The ship was in no great danger, but she had buried herself about twelve feet into the sand. This stuffed up the water intakes and outflows on the ship, making it necessary to extinguish the boilers. Without water, the toilet systems could not be used, making a huge mess aboard for everyone. The date may have had something to do with the grounding. The armistice had been signed the month before and the war was over. It was also New Year's Day and they were only a few hours from landing back in the United States—certainly reasons enough for celebrating.

Coast Guard surfman Roger Smith, patrolling the beach, discovered the 8,255-ton ship on his easterly patrol and signaled her that help was on the way. He then went to the postal telegraph tower and telephoned the station. Captain Louis Pearsall immediately roused his crew, and then called the adjacent stations at Oak Beach and Point o'Woods to muster their crews. He also notified the U.S. Navy radio station at Fire Island.

Aboard ship, Captain Connely sent a message via his shipboard radio through the navy stations at Sayville and Brooklyn informing the navy of the grounding and claiming that all would be evacuated by the next day. That was the second time he was wrong. At 8:00 a.m. the U.S. Coast Guard had its beach apparatus cart opposite the ship and began the job of firing a line across the ship. This was unsuccessful, so the crews went back for the Beebe McLellan surfboat. The two crews, with the help of some of the navy radio operators from the radio communications station, pulled the surfboat to the site. After several attempts, they were successful and a messenger line was rigged.

The next morning, the rescue crew started removing eight to ten of the troops at a time. There were 2,518 passengers aboard, along with a crew of 451. They removed 264 men and women by the end of the day in this way. They were taken across the dunes and put on a ferryboat for Bay Shore. By this time the beach had become a confused madhouse of army and navy reservists sent to help, along with the society ladies from the Red Cross and whatever sightseers managed to sneak onto the beach. The navy had a small fleet of warships offshore and military aircraft were flying over the site. The small private dock at Lonelyville was being guarded by the army and the oceanfront was guarded by the navy. Dockside, there were bales of knitted sweaters, huge stacks of army blankets and tents. Every boat seemed to bring more supplies. The Red Cross ladies had set up and were serving coffee and sandwiches.

When Dr. George King managed to get to his bungalow, he found the front door bashed in and military people serving his tea to some ladies. Later on, he discovered that they had been under the building, found his secret cache of five cases of Hunter whiskey and emptied them. The doctor had put them there as a hedge against the new Volstead Act (Prohibition) that had just been passed by Congress.

The Coast Guard crews working in relays were ferrying people ashore. Many were stretcher cases that were put in wire stretcher baskets along with their mattresses and bedclothes and lowered into the waiting surfboats.

The surf between the ship and shore was often quite rough and several times boats were overturned, dumping rescuers and rescued alike into the cold surf. Those ashore waded or swam out to rescue them. Many needed medical attention. Fortunately, there were no fatalities.

When the wind shifted to an offshore breeze, the one-hundred-foot navy subchasers were able to come alongside the ship and remove one hundred people at a time and take them off to the larger ships waiting farther offshore. From there they were transported to the port of embarkation at Hoboken, New Jersey.

Dr. King had attended every major wreck on the south shore since he was fifteen. He had played hooky from Patchogue High School with another student and headed for the beach in 1893 to watch the events surrounding the wreck of the *Louise H. Randall* at Smith's Point. He worked with the lifesaving crews and was well known to them. During the *Northern Pacific* wreck, he managed to take the place of one of the surfmen and went out to the ship. While waiting for their next load of passengers, he and a couple of the surfmen climbed up the Jacob's ladder to have a look around. The doctor said, "Almost the first person I saw on the boat was a seaman named Thurber, a Bay Shore boy who had joined the Navy. He let out a war hoop and grabbed me in a big bear hug. 'My God, Doc,' he yelled, 'I'm glad to see you. I've stood on the deck of this boat and looked at your bungalow ashore and thought of you many times since we stranded.'"

"How did the ship happen to come ashore?" Dr. King asked, for that was what he really wanted to know all the time. Thurber's reply came,

That is more than I can tell. We were running along and being so close to home I was on deck, although it was not my watch. When I saw the lightship and the lighthouse I knew we were close to shore, and went to the shore side of the ship. There were the beach hills and the surf so close you could almost throw a stone ashore. I rushed up to the bridge and spoke to one of the men on watch and told him we would be aground within a few minutes if the ship's course was not changed. He told me to mind my own damned business and keep off the bridge. I had scarcely reached the deck when I felt the ship slowing down and bumping as she hit the outer bar, and in five minutes, she was fast aground. The officers then reversed the engines and did everything possible to get off, but it was too late.

The removal of the passengers took four days. After that, the baggage was removed. On January 6, wrecking crews moved in to cut and remove her masts and to pump out the remaining fuel oil. By January 18, the tugs were straining to remove her from the twelve feet of sand out to where her twenty-six-foot draft would allow her to float. She came free around 9:00 p.m. and was towed in to the Thirty-fifth Street Brooklyn pier, where it was discovered that she was none the worse for her eighteen days aground on Fire Island.

A court of inquiry was convened aboard on January 21. After four days of testimony, it was the conclusion of the court after going over the navigator's report, which had been checked by the captain, that the navigator had been incorrect in his last astronomical fix, taken 220 miles from the Fire Island Light. In addition, he had not taken into account the set of the current.

The Coast Guard had employed over one hundred of its crews during the long operation. The *Northern Pacific* returned to active service and several years later was completely destroyed by fire while off the New Jersey coast.

Submarines off Long Island: From the Revolutionary War to World War I

EARLY SUBMARINES ON LONG ISLAND WATERS

In 1580, an Englishman, William Bourne, first put forth the idea of a submarine. Many plans and several attempts were made in Europe. In 1776, Yale graduate David Bushnell of Saybrook, Connecticut, built the first submarine to attack an enemy warship. The event took place near Governor's Island, where the fifty-gun British warship *Asia* was anchored.

Bushnell built his submarine with money furnished by General George Washington. It was called the *American Turtle*, and its name was inspired by its shape. The craft floated with only six inches above the water and seven feet below. It was constructed of oak planks bound with iron bands for strength and tarred to make it waterproof. It weighed about a ton! There was room for only one man onboard, and when it was submerged the operator sat on a small shelf looking through five windows the size of half dollars.

Practice took place in Long Island Sound. To descend, the operator stepped on a brass valve, which allowed water to enter a chamber at the bottom of the vessel. To ascend, he operated two brass pumps to force the water out. The strange craft was propelled forward or aft by turning a crank that was attached to two short oars near the front of the submarine. With hard work, the submarine went three knots. The operator (should we call him captain?) steered with a stern tiller with his right hand. By reversing the crank attached to the oars, he could move the craft forward or reverse. He had enough air to stay under for thirty minutes. It was hot, humid and dark.

Bushnell had trained his brother to run the craft, and when the time neared for the mission the brother was taken ill (smart move!). Three volunteers were obtained from the army and trained. Husky, twenty-seven-year-old Sergeant Ezra Lee of Connecticut was picked.

New York Harbor contained about three hundred British warships and New York was a city of about twenty-five thousand residents. The British had defeated the Americans at the battle of Long Island in Brooklyn in August of 1776.

The evening of September 6, 1776, was calm and clear. At almost slack tide, whaleboats towed Lee and the strange craft with muffled oars toward the British warship *Asia*. Attached to the submarine was a waterproof magazine containing 130 pounds of gunpowder equipped with a gun's flintlock to fire the charge and a clock timing mechanism to give Lee about twenty minutes to get away.

The whaleboats towed him as near as they dared and cut him loose. Unfortunately, they had misjudged the tide and he was swept beyond his target. Anyone who has navigated around in lower New York Bay in a small vessel is well aware of the swift tides present.

Sergeant Lee rowed back to his intended target. In a letter to Thomas Jefferson years later, he described what happened when he reached the warship: "When I rowed under the stern of the ship, I could see the men on the deck and hear them talk. I then shut down all the doors, sunk down and came up under the bottom of the ship." When submerged, it was dark inside the submarine, except for a glowing pocket compass near Lee's head, its tip made luminous by foxfire, a glowing fungus found on decayed wood.

It was time to attach the gunpowder magazine to the British ship by means of a large, auger-like screw, a maneuver Lee had practiced in Long Island Sound. The sergeant recalled, "Up with the screw against the bottom but found it would not enter. I pulled along and tried another place, but deviated a little to one side and immediately rose with great velocity and came above the surface two or three feet between the ship and the daylight [silhouetting him], then sunk again like a porpoise. I hove about to try again."

He was shaken by the accidental surfacing and feared being detected. The thought of twenty-five of the fifty cannons aimed at him in close quarters rattled him. The approach of dawn was another factor. He wrote, "On further thought I gave out…and I thought the best generalship was to retreat as fast as I could as I had four miles to go before passing Governor's Island, so I jogged on as fast as I could, and my compass being then of no use to me, I was obliged to rise up every few minutes to see that I sailed in the right direction."

In the smooth water of the dawn, the *American Turtle* left an unusual zigzagged trail that was soon spotted by the British on Governor's Island.

Lee squinted at the Island and said, "300 or 400 men got up on the parapet to observe me, at length a number came down to the shore, shoved off a 12 oared barge with five or six sitters and pulled for me." They got within forty or sixty yards of him before he set the magazine adrift, perhaps hoping they would pick it up and it would explode. However, the British had heard rumors of American experiments with explosives.

Lee recalled, "They took fright and returned to the Island to my infinite joy." Lee cranked away on the oar driver and was met by an American whaleboat, which towed him to safety. Later he recounted, "The magazine after getting a little past the Island, went off with a tremendous explosion, throwing up large bodies of water to an immense height."

Whether they ever tried the submarine again is unknown. The business of submarines seemed to rest until the Civil War came along. Before the war, a few submarine experiments were carried on by the private sector. Both sides experimented with undersea craft. The North publicly denounced the use of such craft while secretly engaging in a building program. All was kept secret and most records were destroyed after the war, so little is known.

The vessel being built by the North had one torpedo tube and some other armament. The Spanish-American War loomed, but the navy still wouldn't buy. By that time, the inventor had moved his operation to Brooklyn. He took an entrepreneur named Isaac Rice for a test ride. He was impressed enough to buy Holland out and start the Electric Boat Company, still in existence in Groton, Connecticut, today.

The boat attracted too much unwanted attention in New York Harbor and a hunt for a new place turned up a boatyard in New Suffolk. The Goldsmith and Tuthill Boatyard was leased for ten dollars a month.

Charles Morris, chief engineer of the Holland Torpedo Boat Company, made arrangements with his new boss to have the boat towed around Orient to New Suffolk. In this area next to Peconic Bay is a plaque stating that on that spot was the first submarine base. There is also a historical marker at the corner of First and Main Streets in Cutchogue, Long Island.

A trial range was set up in Little Peconic Bay with buoys marking the course. Naval officers and VIPs were taken for a ride. On October 11, 1899, a demonstration run was being made by Holland for two U.S. senators and others. A gasket blew and the resulting fumes overcame the crew and guests. The vessel glided, unmanned, into the dock, where employees tied it up and managed to revive everyone. The skipper decided to carry caged mice from then on, stating that when the mice died it was time to go ashore. Miners used canaries in the same way.

The navy was still dubious about the submarine. They had it make a five-hundred-mile inland waterway trip to test it. No one would insure a sea voyage of such a craft. The voyage ended up in Washington, D.C., where the sub was put through trials in the spring of 1900 for an audience of VIPs, including Admiral Dewey of Spanish-American War fame.

The submarine *Holland* was purchased by the navy. The company lost over $80,000 on the deal, but was counting on future sales.

The navy put a crew aboard and made Lieutenant Harry Caldwell the first submarine captain. They put their new submarine right to work in war games off Cape Cod near the Brenton Reef Lightship. In mock games, the *Holland* attacked and "sank" the admiral's flagship, *Kearsage*.

The navy put in an order for six more submarines from the Electric Boat Company. The *Adder*, *Moccasin*, *Porpoise*, *Shark* and *Fulton* were all tested at New Suffolk. In 1905, the company moved to Groton, Connecticut, where it remains today as part of General Dynamics building nuclear submarines.

The navy renamed the *Holland* the *SS1* and used it as a training vessel until 1910. It became a traveling display until 1930, when it was sold for scrap.

By the start of World War I in 1914, the major world powers all had submarines that could deliver torpedoes into large ships. They were often used to lay mines. The harbor entrances to New York were mined during World War I and it is generally accepted that one such mine sunk the USS *San Diego* off Fire Island. The German *U-156* is credited with laying the mines. She disappeared on the homeward trip, believed to be sunk by a mine laid in the North Sea by the U.S. Navy.

At the start of World War II, German submarines were busy within sight of Long Island and other parts of the East Coast. On January 14, 1942, the *Norness* was sunk off Block Island. The next day the *Coimbra* was sunk south of Shinnecock Inlet, both by the *U-123*. *Operation Drumbeat* by Michael Gannon gives a fascinating blow-by-blow description of the submarine operations off our coast in interviews with the German captains.

WORLD WAR I SUBMARINE ATTACKS ON THE U.S. EAST COAST

The German government probably had a more active spy network here in World War II. Saboteurs blew up the munitions arsenal on Black Tom Island in New Jersey, resulting in a $2 million loss.

At Sayville, the German firm Telefunken established a worldwide radiotelegraph service. It was discovered that they were sending high-speed coded messages between the letters of their regular traffic by the use of an automatic keyer. The *Patchogue Advance* on April 20, 1916, reported that sixteen marines from the Brooklyn navy yard arrived and took control of the station. It remained a U.S. Navy station during the war.

Young men rushed to become part of the nation's military. In 1916, the powerboat enthusiasts attempted to form a group to "help" the navy by having built anti-submarine wooden patrol craft, paid for out of their own deep pockets. Five forty-foot vessels with six-cylinder engines were built by members of the Boston Yacht Club. This patrol squadron even managed to take the assistant secretary of the navy, Franklin Delano Roosevelt, for a ride. Boatmen from all over the country had been writing to the secretary of the navy offering similar services. Secretary Daniels arranged a cruise for an East Coast group to last three weeks. They had to pay all their expenses. The navy was to inspect the boats and a naval officer was to be assigned aboard to teach seamanship. The navy preferred boats from sixty-five to one hundred feet long. It rather sounds as if the trip idea was a political ploy, possibly to induce the men to join the naval reserve, which was just being formed. Of course these well-to-do young men could have joined the naval reserve and received commissions, but that would have meant that they couldn't play with their own boats.

Another group was busy organizing a Volunteer Torpedo Patrol within the U.S. Power Squadron. It is doubtful that these efforts could have been much help to the war effort. The deck gun of a surfaced submarine would surely have made short work of these small wooden boats without adequate armament.

By 1917, the navy was building 110-foot wooden subchasers. These were manned by naval reservists and were effective. They had crude, underwater steerable listening devices to detect the direction of enemy subs.

World War I submarines were smaller and quite fragile compared to those used in World War II. Surprisingly, the earlier versions made their way across the Atlantic and were busy in 1918 with their torpedoes, gunfire and TNT sinking ships under our noses.

On Long Island, there has been a lot of interest in the wreck of the USS *San Diego* since its rediscovery in the 1950s. It is currently laying about 110 feet under the surface and has become a favorite dive site. There has always been some question of exactly how she was sunk. It could have been a torpedo or a mine. Initially those aboard thought they spotted a submarine. The best guess is that it was a mine. The *U-156* was a mine-laying submarine operating in the New York traffic lane. Her trip back to Germany was interrupted by a mine in the large minefield planted by the U.S. Navy in the North Sea. She went down with all hands. Radios did not reach across the Atlantic in those days, so there are no records existing of her activities off the East Coast of the United States. The *U-156* carried over one hundred floating mines. She was part of a fleet of seven large submarines ordered to the East Coast to lay mines from Key West to Cape Cod. One of these subs, the *U-155*, was formerly the *Deutschland*, a freight-carrying undersea boat that had visited America before the war.

During World War I, men from the newly formed U.S. Coast Guard were integrated into navy crews. Captain Alex Larzelere in his recent book, *The Coast Guard in World War I*, states unequivocally that the sinking of the USS *San Diego* was the result of a mine. The next day navy minesweepers located six German mines in the area. This was the largest ship lost by the U.S. Navy in the war. There were six deaths at the time and six more deaths of divers aboard the upside-down ship occurred after the fact. Four steamships stopped to help and rescued the rest of the 1,114 crewmen. The 504-foot U.S. armored cruiser sank on July 19, 1918.

A sister sub to the *Deutschland* was the *U-151*, leaving Germany April 18, 1918, arriving off Cape Hatteras on May 21. At night when she surfaced, the crew rigged their wireless antenna and picked up maritime shore stations. The message oft repeated was "No submarines, no war warning." Their first port of call was Delaware Bay and the port of Baltimore, where they were to sow some of their mines. This was done under the cover of darkness. The harbor area was crowded with both commercial traffic and warships. It was a ticklish job to sow the mines and keep from being run down by the heavy traffic.

As they were heading for the next harbor, the three-masted schooner *Hattie Dunn* was spotted. As was the custom at that time, the *U-151* fired a shot across the bow, stopping the ship. Four German sailors took an inflatable over to the ship. At that moment another sailing ship appeared. The captain yelled across to his men to plant the TNT and order the ship's crew to their lifeboats. The second ship, the *Hauppage*, was stopped and the sub's crew got up-to-date area charts and fresh food. The crews of both ships were taken aboard the submarine and the second schooner was blown up with TNT. The German crew felt bad about destroying these fine sailing ships. The next ship to fall prey was the *Edna*. Their crew was taken aboard and the ship sunk. The captain of the *Hattie Dunn* recognized the captain of the *Edna* as a school chum he hadn't seen in thirty years—a rather strange place to meet, aboard a German submarine!

Rudimentary passive sonar was installed on these subs. The captain tells of being able to hear the bell on the Overfalls Lightship. By using a pair of earphones, they could turn the submerged sub so that they knew if the sound was equal in both ears, then they were headed for the lightship.

The *U-151* headed north for the entrance to New York with its captives still aboard. They had onboard a device designed to cut underwater cables by dragging a cable from the surface. Every time the crew spotted a ship, they had to stop and dive out of sight. It was later determined they had managed to cut the cables to South America and one to Europe in the three days that they tried. They also got a good look at the bright nightlights on New York City and they could see the cottages along Fire Island.

From Fire Island, their odyssey took them toward Nantucket and the Gulf of Maine. The captive captains warned the sub skipper of the thick fogs to be encountered in the north at this time of year. The predicted foul weather was found and the *U-151*'s captain decided to head back for Delaware Bay, where there were plenty of targets.

On June 2, a schooner was spotted and they made way toward it. The *Isabel B. Wiley* hove to and awaited her fate. Just then a steamer appeared. A warning shot sounded and she stopped. She was the SS *Winneconne* out of New York. A prize crew brought her to the schooner standing by. The lifeboats from both ships were moored alongside the sub and the twenty-six men were brought aboard. In their three weeks aboard the sub, they had gotten friendly with the German crew and they had made a big dent in the sub's food supplies. They were told to be sure to tell the American newspapers about how well they were treated, as American propaganda had painted the German subs rather blackly. I am sure that the earlier sinking of the *Lusitania* by a German sub had a lot to do with this characterization.

The lifeboats were motorized and would have no trouble reaching shore. By that time, the wireless was reporting submarine activity and warning ships to seek safe harbor. After sinking one more schooner, the *U-151* spotted a troopship. After the lifeboats had gotten away, this ship was sunk by gunfire.

1. Model of twenty-two-gun sloop of war *Sylph*.

2. Memorial to the *Bristol* and the *Mexico*.

3. Margaret Fuller, writer and feminist.

4. The *Franklin*.

5. Schooner *Louise H. Randall*.

6. The old Quogue Life-Saving Station.

7. Picking the bones of the *Augustus Hunt*.

8. The coal schooner *William C. Carnegie*.

9. The stern of the sinking *Northern Pacific*.

10. Lowering a stretcher from the *Northern Pacific*.

11. Lifeboat
lowering from the
Northern Pacific.

12. Loran system, used to determine a ship's position.

13. *Pelican* outbound.

Long Island's Rumrunners and Bootleggers

1920: THE GREAT RUM WAR

The character of the newly formed U.S. Coast Guard was being shaped after "the war to end all wars." The climate of the country was that of turmoil. The troops were brought home, deloused and paraded in public. As they were mustered out, there were suddenly large numbers of men looking for jobs. There was no GI Bill in 1918 to ease their way back into civilian life.

The city people were pitted against country people. There was a wide gap in the way each looked at the rapidly changing society. There were many problems; some of them sound surprisingly modern. There were race riots. The Ku Klux Klan became an evil force, more in rural areas than in the cities. There was a fear of the recent Bolshevik Revolution spreading from Russia.

The fundamentalists from rural areas stirred up hatred. They, along with the Women's Christian Temperance Union and the Anti-Saloon League, managed to influence the Congress to pass the Volstead Act, which provided the enforcement apparatus for the Eighteenth Amendment prohibiting the sale of intoxicating beverages. On

October 28, 1919, the act became the law of the land. The next year, women won their right to vote.

From start to finish, Prohibition was a disaster. Drinking increased among young men and women. Contempt for the law was widespread. Prohibition actually encouraged the very evils that it was meant to destroy. Women were casting off their Victorian clothing and mores. Short skirts, bobbed hair and lipstick were seen on young women both in the streets and in the speakeasies where they danced to the new jazz.

America went into World War I still as a nation of the nineteenth century, and after the war it convulsed into the twentieth century with all the changes in lifestyle, including radio broadcasts to listen to and cars to drive.

Into this mix, the newly formed Coast Guard was suddenly asked to enforce the smuggling law and stop the flow of liquor into the country. Bootlegging gave organized crime an instantly profitable business. Congress had made no plans to hire more customs agents to enforce this new act. Now that liquor was illegal, drinking became the "in" thing to do. When the police, who usually looked the other way, did bring someone in, the judges usually threw the case out.

Coast Guardsmen at that point were paid less than their lifesaving service predecessors had been. Honest jobs were hard to come by, but the easy money that came with the bootlegging reached about everyone along the coastal areas of the country.

The only inlets for laden vessels to pass through on the south shore of Long Island in the 1920s were Fire Island, Jones and Rockaway. In 1931, shortly before the end of Prohibition, the Moriches inlet broke through right between the Moriches Coast Guard Station and the wreck of the *Franklin*.

Fishermen loaded up at mother ships outside the three-mile limit, called rum row, and landed the booze on the beach with their fishing dories. From there it was transported to waiting boats on the bay side and to the docks on the mainland to be unloaded into waiting trucks, which soon delivered it to the speakeasies.

The frame of the engine of the *Franklin*, wrecked in 1854, loomed several feet out of the water less than a mile from the Coast Guard station. The bootleggers had an endless pulley arrangement like a clothesline rigged between the wreck and the shore a hundred yards or so away. Small fishing dories would tie up to the wreck and run the booze in to the waiting crew ashore, thus escaping the necessity of a surf landing with their precious cargo.

What happened to the liquor after it was landed was related to the writer as follows.

> *A fishing boat would pull into the public dock at the foot of Bay Avenue in Eastport, L.I. and unload cases of booze directly into a "borrowed" U.S. mail truck. The driver was handed a bunch of envelopes with numbers on them. As he went on his rounds he would be stopped at police checkpoints. An envelope was handed over and he was allowed to proceed. This continued until all the cases of liquor were delivered. Just about everyone was paid off.*

In this climate, it was no wonder that some of the local Coast Guard surfmen developed cases of night blindness. There were stories of Coast Guard surfboats being used to deliver the illegal cargo. The state police were often on hand ashore to make sure that the illegal liquor wasn't hijacked by a rival gang.

As the war escalated, the Coast Guard had fast boats built in local shipyards around Freeport, Long Island. The bootleggers would have theirs built at the same place, with the proviso that they received the faster boats. It was estimated in 1924 that the Coast Guard was stopping only about 5 percent of the total influx of liquor from all the neighboring countries and most of the European countries. By that time the Coast Guard was able to obtain some seized vessels to use. Usually seized vessels were sold at a government auction and bought back by those who originally owned them. Congressional action resulted in the Coast Guard receiving 20 destroyers, 2 minesweepers and some smaller boats from the navy. Money was appropriated for 323 small, fast boats to be built. With this new fleet, the Coast Guard engaged in many battles, but in the end, only repealing the law solved the problem.

Attempts to board suspected rumrunners often resulted in a chase, with the Coast Guard throwing several shells across the bow of the rummy. If this did not work, officials attempted to disable the vessel by gunfire. There were occasional casualties.

On the afternoon of December 28, 1929, Boatswain Alexander Cornell was underway on the *CG-290*, one of the seventy-five-foot vessels built to help stop the rumrunners, leaving the New London, Connecticut base for a patrol in the eastern passage of Narragansett Bay, jointly with the *CG-241*. Their intention was to prevent any smuggling vessel from entering the area. The skipper had over sixteen years of sea experience in the merchant marine and the navy as well as the Coast Guard. The *CG-290* took up a position near Dumpling Rock in the evening. The *CG-241* was on the other side of the channel near Fort Adams. Meanwhile, the *Black Duck*, a speedboat-type rumrunner, had taken on a load of 383 bags of assorted liquor from the British ship *Symor* and was headed into Narragansett Bay.

The black, as rumrunners were called, was heard faintly at 2:15 a.m. The sea was calm and a patchy fog was present. Under these conditions, sound traveled well.

The *Black Duck* had two three-hundred-horsepower engines, was heavily muffled and was equipped with a smoke screen device. She was very fast and had eluded Cornell for over a year. She was headed into Narragansett Bay with her cargo. As Cornell peered intently into the night, the speedboat suddenly appeared out of the mist moving at high speed without lights. Cornell turned his searchlight on the vessel, instantly recognizing it. Some of the cargo was plainly visible on the deck. He swung his searchlight, alternating between the boat and the Coast Guard ensign, and at the same time sounding his klaxon horn as a signal for her to stop. She passed within seventy-five feet of the bow of the *CG-290*, and as she passed, Cornell used his loudhailer ordering her to stop. No one was visible on her decks. As she was drawing away, Cornell ordered the seaman at the machine gun to open fire. He did so, aiming for the stern of the boat, as was the standard procedure in such cases. His burst consisted of twenty-one shots in about three seconds. At the same time, the *Black Duck* swerved sharply to the left with the result that, instead of going astern, the shots raked the port side of the vessel and hit the pilot house. Then the gun jammed and the *Black Duck* disappeared toward shore.

Shortly thereafter, the black reappeared out of the fog heading for the *CG-290*. She turned on her lights and maneuvered with difficulty next to the Coast Guard boat. The black was then secured to the *CG-290* and boarded. Coast Guardsmen found a man crumpled up on deck near the wheel and two more on the deck of the pilothouse.

The three men were dead and the fourth was wounded in the hand and was given first aid by the Coast Guardsmen.

The *CG-290*, after taking one sack of liquor aboard as evidence, proceeded to Fort Adams with the *Black Duck* in tow. The three men were pronounced dead by a doctor and the fourth was treated.

A Coast Guard Board of Investigation cleared Cornell and the gunner of any wrongdoing. Later, a special grand jury at Providence, Rhode Island, also cleared them. The *Black Duck* was turned over to the Coast Guard and became the *CG-808*. The public, however, was not as forgiving. Shortly thereafter, a protesting mob tore down recruiting posters in Boston. In New London, a gang brutally beat up two Coast Guardsmen, resulting in fines for three of the attackers. Boatswain Cornell was one of the most outstanding skippers of the rum war, with over ten captures to his credit.

1929: THE CASE OF THE *BEATRICE K* AND OTHER BOOTLEGGING STORIES OFF LONG ISLAND

One December day in 1929, Boatswain Cornell in the *CG-290*, a seventy-five-foot Coast Guard cutter, finished his patrol of Gardiner's Bay at nightfall. He anchored near the entrance of Shelter Island Sound just north of Noyac Bay. The vessel was hard to spot against the black shoreline. After only an hour's wait, a vessel approached with no lights showing. The *CG-290* weighed anchor and as the darkened vessel passed, she went in pursuit at full throttle. The patrol boat pulled alongside, ordering the other vessel to halt. As the vessels came together, the *CG-290* split a wooden railing on the suspect vessel. The rummy was ordered to anchor.

This was the same Boatswain Cornell who had been involved earlier in the unfortunate incident with the shooting deaths of three rumrunners aboard the *Black Duck*. By this time (1929–30), most people were really fed up with Prohibition. The newspapers were playing up incidences of the Coast Guard's use of arms while enforcing this immensely unpopular law. This case was even debated by Congress, where the "wets" took umbrage and the "drys" defended the actions.

Captain O. Nelson identified his vessel as the *Beatrice K* out of Gloucester. He produced papers, including a license for mackerel and cod fishing. The vessel was boarded by two Coast Guardsmen. While they were searching, Nelson decided to act friendly and talked to Boatswain Cornell. He related how he had been boarded by the destroyer *Fanning* and given a clean bill of health after a thorough search. Nelson claimed that he had sixty thousand pounds of fish aboard for New York and that they would spoil if he were detained. He said that his generator had broken down and his batteries were dead, which was the reason he was running without lights, and that the *Beatrice K* was leaking badly. He claimed to be a stranger to the area and had picked Sag Harbor as a likely place for repairs. Further talk revealed that he had been fishing off George's Bank for fifteen years. The men searching the suspected boat's hold said that it contained fish and ice.

Cornell thought things over and decided that some things did not ring quite true. No liquor had been found, but why would a ship needing repairs go twenty miles out of her way while passing up the facilities available at New Bedford, Newport or New London, all of which were nearer? The batteries were found to be perfectly dry, indicating that they had been dumped out. When asked why there was a bucket over the exhaust, the captain became angry and threw the bucket over the side, but he did not seem to mind the split rail. Cornell just could not believe anyone fishing George's Banks for fifteen years would be so unfamiliar with Long Island Sound. Acting on his suspicions, Cornell decided that the vessel needed to be searched more thoroughly, so after placing a man aboard, he ordered the *Beatrice K* to proceed to New London.

At base four her holds were opened and the fish and ice were removed. About eighteen inches down there was a layer of tarpaper, and under it were uncovered 1,600 sacks of Meadville pure rye whiskey! When the booze was found and Cornell addressed Nelson as "captain," Nelson replied, "Don't call me captain, I am not the captain, he left in a dory before you came on board." The crew was arrested and the vessel was seized for probable cause. Cornell received a commendation from the base commander and a Commandant's Letter of Commendation for his actions.

This "watertight" case went to trial and the judge held that the Coast Guard had no right to arrest the crew of the *Beatrice K* for running without lights and no right to search the vessel without a search warrant. He agreed with the defense attorneys that the vessel was the "home" of the crewmembers and was inviolable for the purpose of an extensive search. The *Beatrice K* was released on bond and the crew was found not guilty. It was a ridiculous ruling, but it stood. This aroused the indignation of Coast Guard officers far and wide because it meant that this case could be used to obtain the release of other vessels that might be seized.

This case pointed out the frustration of the Coast Guard working against most of the citizens of the country, who wanted their liquor. The system bred corruption at all levels. In these lean years, most everyone was either on the take or actively involved in bootlegging, the most profitable business for those making their living on and around the sea.

Long Island during Prohibition was a broad highway from Montauk to Manhattan over which trucks, cars and anything that would roll were headed west toward the city with their liquid cargo of distilled spirits and wines. Just about every creek, dock or landing of any sort was used at one time or another to land the illicit liquor. Ships from Europe and Canada hung out offshore in international waters. Anything that floated—speedboats with large engines designed for the purpose down to craft under sail—was used to transport from the mother ships to trucks waiting ashore. Sometimes large private yachts, painted white, were spotted with telltale black scratches in their fine paint, indicating that they had been alongside a large ship.

Of course, not all of the liquor went to New York City. There were plenty of local watering holes most anywhere on Long Island. The local police could close them under a public nuisance law, which was only a misdemeanor. If offenders were making their own booze in the bathtub, then the feds could crack down on them with more serious charges.

In 1929 and 1930, Suffolk County on Long Island had a district attorney by the name of Alexander G. Blue. He set out to vigorously enforce the liquor laws. From reading the newspaper accounts in the *Patchogue Advance*, one is left with the conclusion that he might have been unpopular with everybody!

In March 1930, Blue and sheriff's deputies seized a truckload of liquor and proceeded to smash the contents. The federal officers accused him of improperly destroying evidence that was supposed to go into a federal warehouse in Brooklyn. Blue accused them of "losing" a quantity of the cargo on the way to the warehouse. On the same night the Coast Guard seized a truckload of booze worth over $10,000 near the Napeague Coast Guard Station, near Montauk. The driver escaped.

The February 11, 1930 edition of the *Patchogue Advance* is headlined with "Boatload of Rum Is Caught in Ice." When the bay froze over, liquor was suddenly in short supply. A speedboat had attempted to bring in a load and was caught in quick-forming ice between Gilgo and Oak Island. The crew of five was working on the speedboat *Edith*, believed to be owned by a Boston syndicate. The Coast Guard had spotted the distressed vessel from the station and set out to rescue the crew. While on their way, they saw the *Doris V* out of East Islip, Long Island, reach the crew and take them aboard.

When the Coast Guardsmen reached the *Edith*, they found her loaded with five hundred cases of "champagne, cordials, and whiskey." About seventy-five more cases were found partly frozen in the ice where they had been jettisoned to lighten the boat. The Coast Guard crew notified the icebreaker at Bay Shore to apprehend the *Doris V*. They caught up to her near Sayville. The men were transported to Brooklyn for arraignment in federal court and the liquor was brought to the federal impound. The men were bailed out with bail set at $2,500 each. They were met by a syndicate lawyer and bondsman, who took care of their cases.

A few days later, the *Nautis* ran aground four miles from Montauk Point between Block Island and Gardiner's Island, but the crew escaped in a small boat. The Coast Guard found three hundred cases onboard and some floating about where an attempt had been made to get rid of the evidence. The boat was taken to New London and impounded.

Rumrunners were not happy with people who informed on them. On January 10, 1930, the *Patchogue Advance* reported that a man and his family living on the Patchogue River were run off their own property by two armed men. The head of the household found his telephone wires cut in two places and appealed to the police for protection. He found a note in his mailbox threatening to bomb his house. His family moved out after that. The bootleggers had been raided at a dock nearby previously, and evidently they suspected him of reporting their actions.

When you see an old-timer at your local marina, you might just go up to him and ask about the rumrunning days. Most of the participants are now gone, but the stories remain. After Prohibition was repealed, the subject was taboo. Not many liked to talk of the "old days" because it often involved friends, relatives and neighbors in this illegal business.

World War II off Long Island

WAR COMES TO LONG ISLAND: THE SINKING OF THE *COMBRIA*

On December 7, 1941, the Japanese attacked Pearl Harbor in faraway (it seemed at the time) Hawaii. By January, German submarines were operating right off our coastline. They were so close, in fact, that one of them actually ran aground near Rockaway, but managed to get away undetected. On January 15, 1942, at 1:40 a.m., a torpedo hit the 423-foot, 6,700-ton tanker *Combria*. The sinking resulted in the captain and thirty-five of the crew being burned to death.

The ship was British, built in Germany before the war. She was loaded with light lubricating oil. She was lit up with her peacetime lights showing. The lights of Long Island's shoreline also silhouetted her. The reality of war hadn't struck home yet with the military or civilian officials. All lighted aids to navigation on the East Coast were operating as if we were still at peace.

Kapitänleutnant Reinhard Hardegen, commanding the *U-123*, placed one torpedo amidships and the tanker lit up the sky with flames. Hardegen saw the gun crew running for the stern gun on the tanker and decided to expend another torpedo because his sub was lit up from the burning oil. The second torpedo sunk the ship, leaving a portion of the bow sticking out of the water.

The burning oil also lit up the shoreline near Shinnecock, resulting in many calls to police and the Coast Guard. Surfboats left from Quogue and Shinnecock stations on their rescue mission.

The Quogue Coast Guard Station later told the press that one of its patrol planes had spotted survivors in a dory and on a raft about twenty-three miles off Shinnecock Inlet and had dropped food and whiskey to them. Whiskey was thought to be a restorative. Both Shinnecock's and Quogue's Coast Guard surfboats launched into the rough seas and were whipped by a cold northeast wind severe enough to keep the fishing fleet in port. One boat was launched as far away as Long Beach, but it returned with a broken prop blade.

During that time the Coast Guard would have had a thirty-six-foot motor surfboat at Shinnecock because of ocean access through the inlet. Quogue, on the other hand, would have had a surfboat and seven oars to be launched through the surf. Navy destroyers 402 and 435, which had been directed to the scene, picked up the six men adrift in the lifeboat by the patrol aircraft.

The *U-123* was part of a small fleet of submarines sent over by the German high command as soon as the war started. The *U-123* left the submarine pens at Lorient, France, on December 23, 1941, complete with a small Christmas tree. She returned for torpedoes and re-provisioning on February 9, 1942.

Adolf Hitler had the German general staff work on plans to invade the United States as early as 1937. In 1940, he planned to capture the Azores to use as a takeoff point for his air force to bomb the East Coast of the United States. In February of 1941, Hitler ordered Admiral Donitz to study the feasibility of U-boat attacks on East Coast navy bases. The admiral believed that the U.S. Navy installations along the East Coast were in such a poor state of readiness that a U-boat could steam directly into the throat of New York Harbor unchallenged. He was right, of course.

During the early part of the war it was rumored that a German sub had been captured and Bond bread wrappers from New York were found in the galley. From my own observation, German naval officers could have roamed the streets of New York without being noticed because the streets were full of uniformed men from every Allied navy in the world. They might only have had to remove insignia containing swastikas.

Admiral Karl Donitz wanted a fleet of three hundred U-boats to stop the flow of supplies to England. In 1939, when the war started, he had fifty-seven U-boats, of which forty-six were seaworthy. Hitler understood land war, but he never understood the need to cut enemy supply lines at sea. He ignored requests for more subs. If he had given his navy the three hundred subs, it would have been a different war.

On December 12, 1941, when the seaborne blitzkrieg was ordered, Donitz had only five U-boats to send to the United States to sink ships before they got far into the shipping lanes. The tactic was called Operation Paukenschlag (Drumbeat). In the first twenty-six days, those five U-boats sank twenty-five ships!

The *Combria* was the third kill for the *U-123*. The first was *Cyclops*, an ancient freighter carrying general cargo from Panama to Halifax, Nova Scotia. After the torpedoing, the *U-123* came to the surface and attempted to take out the ship's radio with its machine gun. The ship was transmitting "SSS," indicating a submarine attack, and giving their position, which also gave away the submarine's position.

The *U-123* was ordered to sink shipping within a box that covered the area from North Carolina to Cape Cod. The next ship encountered was the *Norness*, sunk off Block Island January 14, 1942. All aboard survived the torpedoing.

This sinking was widely reported in the press. The *Combria* sinking the next day led to a confusion of reports as censorship began to be imposed. It took several more sinkings for the U.S. Navy to wake up to the cold fact that there were submarines right on our coastline. The front was here!

British intelligence was well developed by that time and knew approximately where each German submarine was. This information was forwarded to Admiral King, in charge of the U.S. Navy. He chose to ignore any information the British gave. They had a highly developed intelligence system along with a high-frequency direction finding system that tracked German submarines. They had learned from their experiences since the beginning of the war in 1939. The British wanted a convoy system set up with navy ships guarding them. The tremendous losses incurred in the opening months forced the decision on him.

The Germans kept in contact with their command back in Lorient, France, by short, encoded message traffic transmitted on schedule.

The British at Bletchley Park kept careful track of the messages. The capture of the German Enigma machine from a sinking submarine allowed them to decode these messages.

The *U-123* was a type IXB U-boat, 252.5 feet long with a beam of 22.3 feet. The ship could travel on the surface at 18 knots maximum driven by two large diesel engines. At 12 knots she had a cruising range of 8,700 nautical miles. Submerged, the speed using electric motors was 7.3 knots. At 4 knots the maximum range was 64 miles. The submarine had to be surfaced for seven hours to fully recharge the batteries. This submarine type carried a complement of 52. They all shared in the use of the one head. Beside their uniforms, the men were allowed two changes of underwear, one set for outbound and the other for homebound. In addition, they were allowed a sweater and a toothbrush. No one shaved on patrol.

If they were forced to stay submerged for a long period of time and the carbon dioxide had built up and had to be removed, everyone had to breathe through potassium cartridges to neutralize the exhaled gas. While underwater, those not working went to their bunks to conserve oxygen.

The officers' wardroom consisted of four private bunks, two on each side. The upper bunks could be folded up so the lowers could be used as seats. There was a table that folded down and the officers ate there. The captain's bunk was opposite the radio room. His was different from the others in that he had a green curtain for privacy and a foldaway writing table.

The Bible of the U-boat captain was the U-boat Commander's Handbook. This book was a practical distillation of the experiences of commanders who had been in command of a submarine. It told exactly what to do in each case. It was memorized and followed. It made battle decisions easy. The U.S. Navy reprinted it in English after the capture of an intact U-boat.

In 1967, there was a movement to check old sunken tankers for oil leaks that were thought to be contaminating Long Island beaches. The *Combria* was checked in 182 feet of water and almost no leakage was found, probably due to the fact that she was carrying oil that would have surfaced and evaporated. Her position today can be seen on chart 12300 at Loran 26203.5 and 43576 (lat 40°23'2", long 72°21'5". A shipwreck is marked on the chart in that area.

NAZI AGENTS ARRIVE AT AMAGANSETT, LONG ISLAND, BY SUB

The Japanese bombing of Pearl Harbor on December 7, 1941, launched the United States into the global conflict. German submarines were soon busy off the East Coast sinking ships loaded with supplies for the war effort in Europe. America was just waking up to the fact that the war was right here. The Coast Guard had reopened the surf stations that had been closed by the Depression and the Coast Guard's usual lack of funds.

The beach at Amagansett, Long Island, was covered by a heavy fog as twenty-one-year-old Boatswain's Mate Second Class John C. Cullen left the station for the midnight east beach patrol on the night of June 13, 1942. He was armed with nothing but a flashlight, which was not much help in the fog.

Some of the people living along the beach heard noises that sounded like a ship aground. No one investigated; after all, the Coast Guard was on duty. Besides, it was probably them drilling with their boat. What they heard was in actuality the *U-202* aground outside the surf line. She had been caught by the outer bar that had caught so many ships since the 1600s. The U-boat got free with the incoming tide and managed to get offshore far enough that she was not spotted when the fog lifted. What she did leave behind was the strong smell of diesel fumes and four saboteurs.

Lieutenant Commander Lindner of the Nazi submarine *U-202* was glad to rid his ship of the four passengers and resume his regular job of sinking Allied shipping. He found and sank the *City of Birmingham* off Long Island on July 1.

The four passengers were George Dasch, Ernest Burger, Richard Quirin and Heinrich Heinck. They had in common the fact that all had immigrated to the United States and returned to Germany in 1939, when Chancellor Adolf Hitler offered Germans living abroad free passage home. They all had held nondescript jobs in America, none being very successful. George Dasch usually worked as a waiter and mastered the English language better than the others. They, along with four others, were contacted by Walter Kappe, who also had lived in the United States and had been active in the German-American Bund. He had tried unsuccessfully to take Fritz Kuhn's place as head of the Bund.

In Germany, Walter Knappe became part of Abwehr II, the German military intelligence corps. He was given free reign to recruit and train saboteurs. To this end he established a school to train his recruits in the fine art of sabotage. His first project was dubbed "Operation Pastorius." He had been interviewing prospective members of his team and had assembled them at the school, where they went through an intensive three-week training. Their job was to blow up aluminum manufacturing plants, power plants, waterworks, bridges and railroad systems.

Amazingly, what he had assembled was the worst bunch of nonprofessional misfits. Three weeks of training really was not long enough for the raw recruits. They were split into two groups. Dasch was picked to lead both groups. The second group of four was landed by the *U-584* south of Jacksonville, Florida.

When they were ready to leave on the two submarines, Kappe distributed $180,000 in American money to the two groups. Herbert Haupt, from the second group on *U-584*, looked at one of the bills closely and discovered to his horror that it was a gold certificate, all of which had been removed from circulation by the Treasury Department during the Depression, when the United States went off the gold standard. They quickly divested themselves of the gold certificates and the group became worried after Kappe made light of the incident. They wondered what other blunders had been made. Dasch and Burger were paired, as were Quirin and Heinck. All had relatives and friends in the United States.

Under cover of the fog, the submarine worked its way in as close to the beach as the captain dared. The four passengers had with them watertight boxes packed with explosives and timing mechanisms and duffle bags of civilian clothing. They were dressed in navy fatigues so if they were discovered right away they would be treated as prisoners of war.

The four men, along with two crewmen from the sub and all the gear, were loaded into an inflated rubber boat. The two sailors rowed in to the beach with a line attached to the sub trailing behind. Everyone got thoroughly wet landing in the surf. The plan was to change into American clothes and send the German uniforms back with the boat. The boxes were to be buried and recovered later. As Dasch glanced down the beach, he was horrified to see a man walking toward him! Quietly, he told the two sailors to return to the ship and then walked toward the stranger. He claimed that they were fishermen who had come ashore and were waiting for daylight to return to Southampton. One of Dasch's men called out in German to him. The foreign language made Coast Guardsman Cullen suspicious. The men were invited to go back to the station with Cullen to wait for dawn in comfort. By that time, Dasch was groping for a way out of his situation. It was at that point that he threatened Cullen and at the same time offered him a $300 bribe.

They exchanged false names, and Cullen took the money and ran for the Amagansett Coast Guard Station. He knew that there was more than one of the German strangers and that they were unarmed.

The Germans finished burying the boxes and they also buried the duffle bag with the uniforms. They made their way to the Amagansett Railroad Station to await the morning train for New York. The station agent was used to having fishermen seek a train ride in damp, rumpled clothing. The group planned to arrive at Jamaica and go off to buy better clothes and suitcases in order to check into New York hotels.

Back at the Amagansett Station, Cullen was in charge while the chief was off station. The chief was summoned and eventually Coast Guard intelligence in New York was notified. A crew from the station armed themselves and returned to the scene on the beach. They were able to see where the heavy cases had been dragged across the sand and managed to recover them. Coast Guard intelligence officers arrived the next day and took everything to the barge office in lower Manhattan, where the FBI was called in to examine the contents.

The Florida group landed without incident and made its way to Jacksonville. There the men boarded a train for Chicago, their goal.

George Dasch had made up his mind that his best interests would be served if he called the FBI and told them the whole story. Soon after arriving in New York City, he called the New York office of the FBI and told the agent that he would report directly to J. Edgar Hoover and to notify Washington that he was on his way. The agent recorded the conversation but did not pay much attention to it. He was used to receiving crackpot calls. For some reason, the agent was unaware of the Amagansett landing.

Dasch had met up with some of his waiter buddies in the hotel and enjoyed himself playing cards with them. He had sounded out

Burger, who was sharing a room with him, and told him of his plans. Burger had no confidence in Dasch's ability to carry out the task at hand and looked at the surrender as a way out of a bad situation.

Dasch arrived in Washington on Thursday, June 18. He was a bit confused as to who to contact and how to accomplish his task. When he finally called the FBI, they sent a car for him. By this time, they were well aware of the landing. Dasch wanted to tell his long story directly to Hoover, but that did not happen right away. He was permitted to tell his story in his own way, except the FBI agents had to interrupt him from time to time to keep him on track, as he had a tendency to wander off the subject. He wanted to be permitted to meet Kerling at the agreed-to meeting place on July 4. What Dasch had to say at that time filled 254 typewritten pages.

The FBI had its own ideas on how to apprehend the other potential saboteurs. They moved quickly to pick up the men. Six were in custody before Dasch was finished with his long, rambling story.

All of the men had contacted old friends and boasted of their arrival by submarine and their mission. So much for keeping it all a secret! All were carrying money belts with $4,000 on which to live. The minimum wage in the United States at that time was $0.40 an hour, or $16, for a forty-hour week before taxes.

Haupt had left his home in Chicago previously after his girlfriend became pregnant. He took off to Mexico and received money from the German consulate for his trip to Germany. He and several other Germans boarded a ship for Japan, where they transferred to another ship, eventually arriving in Germany.

After a reunion with his parents, he learned that his girlfriend, Gerda Melind, had miscarried. He proposed marriage to her but she was a bit suspicious after previously being abandoned. He also bought a new Pontiac convertible and took steps to evade the draft. Each of the men made their way back to friends and family so they could blend in. They were to meet on July 4 and plan their next move.

On Sunday morning, June 28, 1942, the *New York Sunday News* carried the headline, "German Spies land on L.I.; F.B.I. seizes 8." The story had been held back by the FBI since the landings. During World War II, military censorship was a fact of life.

The Justice Department realized that neither secrecy nor the death penalty could be guaranteed in a civil trial. Attorney General Francis

Biddle conferred with representatives from the War Department and between them came up with a plan to try the men by a military commission under the rules of courts-martial for military personnel. President Franklin D. Roosevelt approved the plan and moved quickly to implement it.

The precedent dated back seventy-seven years to when seven men and one woman were charged with conspiring with John Wilkes Booth to assassinate President Abraham Lincoln. That was the last time civilians had been tried by a military commission in the United States. Given the mood of the country, it was necessary for Roosevelt to move ahead with speed. He issued the order on July 8, 1942, creating the commission.

The president would make the final decision on the sentence after the trial and the commission's recommendations were sent to him. There would be no appeal. The press objected to the secrecy of the trial. The public was told very little. The prisoners were held in separate cells with no means of communication to anyone except their court-appointed army officer lawyers. They were told nothing.

The trial took place on the fifth floor of the Justice Department building in Washington, D.C., in a refurbished assembly room used for training. Heavy drapes were hung, completely cutting off the outside. The trial took just eighteen days. The secrecy was maintained not only throughout the trial, but also for eighteen years thereafter. The three-thousand-page trial transcript remained classified until 1960.

On Saturday, August 8, 1942, six of the prisoners were executed in the electric chair, starting at noon. It was all over by 1:20 p.m. The White House was called and a statement was issued that six had been executed and Burger had received a life sentence. Dasch had been sentenced to thirty years of hard labor. The reporters waiting at the jail had been kept in the dark and found out at the same time as everyone else. The families of those imprisoned were not even told. It had been less than two months from landing to execution.

The story was soon lost in the headlines proclaiming the marine landing at Guadalcanal. Nine weeks after the executions there was a story about the six men being buried in the District of Colombia's Potters Field.

The internment of the Japanese-Americans on the West Coast took place around this time, brought on by unreasonable fears of the populous and the desire to appear to be doing something. The worst that happened to German and Italian Americans, other than surveillance, was to require that their radios have the short-wave coils removed. It all goes under the heading of war hysteria.

Considering the personalities of the men involved in the sub landing, it is doubtful if their mission would have been much of a success even if Dasch had followed orders. The men were not well trained and would have probably eventually tipped their hand to the FBI.

The use of a military tribunal was probably due the tenor of the times. The Pearl Harbor bombing had just precipitated a war on two fronts. President Roosevelt probably felt that the country needed a positive boost of morale. A quick trial and executions would do that. In the same page of the Sunday *News*, there was a story of General Doolittle being honored for leading a raid on Tokyo. The raid was conducted from a carrier at great risk. The planes had to land in China, as they were too large to land on the carrier from which they left. The whole operation was a propaganda coup. It showed the Japanese that they were vulnerable to attack and at the same time was a big morale booster on the homefront.

In 1948, President Truman commuted the sentences of Dasch and Burger and had them deported to Germany. George Dasch was a self-centered individual. What made him betray "Operation Pastorius" was never ascertained. The fact that he could be identified by Coast Guardsman Cullen may have pushed him over the edge. He, however, stuck to his story that he was just using this means to gain reentry into the country.

Dasch wrote an autobiography as an attempt to explain his actions after his release in 1948. He went to the trouble of looking up people who had known him and his alleged anti-Nazi activities in Germany and getting their sworn depositions to prove the point. He was not welcomed in postwar Germany, where he was considered a traitor.

THE LAST BATTLE OFF LONG ISLAND OF WORLD WAR II

The spring of 1945 found the war in Europe winding down. The Allies were marching through Germany, as were the Russians. The submarine menace on the East Coast had diminished considerably.

The navy, however, was still aware of enemy subs in the area. By that time, wartime advances in electronic warfare made it easier to track the enemy subs.

ULTRA, the system of naval intelligence, was able to track enemy naval units. The information input was sightings, sinkings and HF/DF, a system of long-range, high-frequency direction finder stations circling the Atlantic Ocean. One such station was located in Amagansett, Long Island.

German naval units were required to report in with encrypted movement reports. When the subs surfaced and sent their reports, the Huff Duff units, as they were called, discovered their positions. Much of the text could be decoded due to an early capture by the British of the famous Enigma machine. With this information, the U.S. Navy was aware of the *U-853* operating between Montauk and Maine.

On April 23, 1945, the *U-853*, while operating off the Maine coast, spotted a slow moving target. It turned out to be the U.S. Navy's *Eagle PE-56*, a leftover from World War I. No longer suitable as a subchaser, this class of ship was being used as utility boats. The ship was sunk by the *U-853* with thirteen survivors of the sixty-two souls onboard. The destroyer *Selfridge DD-357* dropped depth charges on a possible target after rescuing the survivors.

The navy convened a court of inquiry and concluded that the ship had suffered a boiler explosion, which caused the sinking. This misinformation was to cover up the fact that the navy was aware of the submarine activity.

The survivors remembered seeing a sub surface as they were abandoning ship. They even remembered the conning tower painted with a trotting red horse and yellow shield. Through the tireless research of Paul Lawton of Brockton, Massachusetts, a diver and amateur naval historian, the case was reopened almost forty years later. The navy reclassified the sinking as a combat loss and recommended that Purple Hearts be awarded to its forty-nine dead and thirteen survivors. The ceremony took place in June 2001 aboard the museum ship USS *Salem* in Quincy, Massachusetts. Three of the survivors were present, along with many of the next of kin.

Evidently, the *U-853*, aware that the sinking had alerted the U.S. Navy of its presence, spent a lot of time out of sight on the bottom. A submerged German submarine in World War II could not receive any radio messages. Meanwhile, on April 30, 1945, Adolf Hitler designated Admiral Donitz as his successor and then committed suicide. On May 4, Donitz issued orders that all German forces would surrender. U-boat headquarters sent the following message (translated): "ALL U-BOATS. ATTENTION ALL U-BOATS, CEASE FIRE AT ONCE. STOP ALL HOSTILE ACTION AGAINST ALLIED SHIPPING. DONITZ." There were forty-nine U-boats at sea at that time and several of them were submerged and would not receive the message. Among them, it appears, was the *U-853*.

Meanwhile, the SS *Black Point* was making its way toward Boston with seven thousand tons of coal aboard. She was an old coal-burning ship built in 1918 and was used in the coastal convoys along the East Coast. By 1945 the voyages were thought to be so safe that the captain didn't even post lookouts.

At about 5:40 p.m. on May 5, 1945, the lookout at Point Judith lighthouse noted the *Black Point* as she passed within three miles of his position. At that time, he heard the explosion caused by an acoustic torpedo hitting the stern of the ship. Luke Pelletier, a member of the navy gun crew, started for the ancient Spanish-American War relic gun and discovered that the stern was gone! The Yugoslavian freighter *Kamen* saw the explosion and relayed an SOS immediately. The ship's captain took a chance the sub was not laying in wait for a rescue ship and moved in to rescue the sailors in the water. They were later transported to shore by Coast Guard crash boats.

The *Black Point* sank in fifteen minutes, taking twelve men of the crew with her. The ship's complement consisted of forty-one merchant seamen and five naval armed guards.

The Eastern Sea Frontier headquarters, having received the SOS report and a visual report from the Point Judith light, dispatched orders to naval units within the area. There were several warships headed for the Charlestown Naval Shipyard for work after an Atlantic crossing. These included the destroyer *Erickson DD-440* and the destroyer escorts *Amick DE-168* and *Atherton DE-169*. The patrol frigate *Moberly PF-63* was present and manned by a Coast Guard crew. All ships were diverted to assist in destroying the submarine. Additionally, the navy dispatched two navy blimps from the Lakehurst Naval Air Station in New Jersey. The task group commander was Commander Francis C.B. McCune, aboard the destroyer *Erickson*. The ship was about to enter the Cape

Cod ship canal with a Coast Guard pilot aboard and could not reach the scene for some time. That left Coast Guard Commander Tollasksen as the senior officer present and de facto commander of the task force. He sent all hands to battle stations as the group proceeded to sweep the area for the sub. The *Erickson* was ordered back to the task force and Commander McCune took back his command upon his arrival. As they formed a line about three thousand yards apart, the active sonars were turned off on all ships except the *Atherton*, which was equipped with superior equipment. Other ships could hear the return pings from the *Atherton*'s equipment. Contact was maintained between ships on their TBS bridge-to-bridge radios. All agreed that they had sonar contact with a sub. Depth charges and hedgehog ordnance was loosed on the enemy. The attacks brought up oil and debris. Once again the task force loosed ordnance in the area of the sonar contact. Everyone wanted to get in the act. I guess with the war over, it would save them the trouble of unloading all their munitions.

By that time the navy blimps were overhead and, using MAD, they determined that there was no movement and dropped dye markers in the vicinity of the debris. The airships then added six rocket bombs to the onslaught. Ships crisscrossed the area dropping depth charges and then launching whaleboats to collect debris.

The next day, after the warships had left, the navy ship *Penguin ASR-12*, a rescue vessel, arrived with divers. They were unable to penetrate the sub with their hard hat diving gear, but they reported only two holes in the side. This was after 195 depth charges, 264 hedgehog projectiles and 6 rocket bombs were dropped. This shows how difficult it was to really kill a submarine.

A marker buoy was placed 99° true, 14,000 yards east of Sandy Point Light on Block Island (lat 41°15'55"N, long 71° deg 04'8"W).

Not all the *U-853*'s crew remained aboard; one German sailor's remains came to the surface and drifted to the Rhode Island coast. He was interred at the Rhode Island Cemetery Annex. On the third Sunday of November 2001, several German and American naval personnel gathered at the gravesite to pay respects to the unknown sailor. The third Sunday in November is the German traditional day to honor the military dead.

Ralph DiCarpio says in his story, *The Battle of Point Judith*, "The location of the *U-853* was determined precisely in April 1953 when divers from the destroyer *Samuel B. Roberts DD-823* reached the submarine. It was found resting on the bottom at approximately 130 feet where it remains today having become a popular destination for divers. Unfortunately, there have been several incidents of bones being removed and either taken from the scene, or carelessly tossed back into the water."

Long Island Wrecks in the Modern Age

PELICAN DISASTER AT MONTAUK

On Saturday, September 1, 1951, the party boat *Pelican II* was getting ready for a fishing trip off Montauk Point. The wind was blowing and the Weather Bureau forecast called for small craft warnings. Recreational fishermen from around Long Island and from New York were out for the Labor Day weekend of fishing. Many arrived by car. Witnesses reported that there were thirty to thirty-five people onboard the *Pelican* when the Long Island Railroad's Fisherman's Special pulled in and the amateur fishermen poured onto the waiting party boats. About another thirty boarded the *Pelican*. It was so crowded that several talked about finding a less crowded boat, but the fear of not being able to find a boat led them to stay.

Here is a recent quotation from Captain Frank Mundus, whose charter boat *Cricket II* was tied up right next to the *Pelican*.

> *Everybody's boat was overloaded from commuters off the "Fishermen's Special" and the* Pelican *was the last boat to leave the dock. As my boat was leaving the dock, I looked back and could see the people throwing their fishing tackle down into my cockpit and jumping the five*

feet from the dock to the cockpit deck. I heard Captain Eddie hollering to the people "no more! No more!" Eddie left within minutes of me.

Captain Edward H. Carroll of Staten Island got the forty-two-foot *Pelican* underway around 8:30 a.m. with sixty-two passengers and a mate, who was actually a short-order cook. The ship carried eighty-six life jackets, which were stowed in the cabin. Only one passenger was wearing one, much to the merriment of the others. The boat arrived at Frisbie's fishing bank off the Ditch Plains Coast Guard Station around 10:00 a.m. Upon arrival, the engines were shut down so the passengers could drift for fish. Witnesses testified that it was so crowded that there was no room at the rail to fish. They were told that space would open up soon as the seasick passengers moved away.

The rough weather caused about twenty-five people to seek refuge from the elements in the cabin below; most of them had gotten seasick and wanted to return. There was no panic. They had been fishing about a mile southeast of Montauk Point when the captain attempted to restart his engines. He found that both refused to start. The captain's aide was of no help, so the captain worked on the engines. He was finally able to restart one engine. He started back with forty-mile-per-hour winds and a riptide around the point that slowed him down.

Running on one one-hundred-horsepower engine resulted in covering only six miles in two and a half hours. By that time, the vessel was side to the wind, causing it to rock from side to side, at one point keeling over almost sixty degrees. The weather calmed down after that for a bit, then the weather worsened again and the *Pelican* rolled again. This time she capsized, trapping many of the cold, seasick passengers, including women and children, in the cabin. Many of the bodies were recovered after the capsized vessel was towed back to the docks before dawn Sunday morning.

The two vessels closest to the scene were the pleasure craft *Betty Jane* operated by Howard Bishop, a naval reservist, and the charter boat *Bingo II*, operated by Lester Behan, a Coast Guard auxiliarist. Bishop was able to retrieve six people. He had considerable difficulty because the only persons aboard his boat were elderly. Persons in the water were unable to help themselves and their dead weight had to be pulled up and over the rail of the rescuing craft. Both boats, upon arriving on scene, immediately threw lifejackets and anything that would float in the water for the drowning people to grab. The *Bingo II* arrived second and proceeded to rescue twelve people. Both boats had difficulty in maneuvering with rough seas and people in the water. In the twenty-five minutes that the rescuing boats were working, they had drifted some distance from the hulk of the *Pelican*. About 3:15 p.m., the Coast Guard picket boat from Ditch Plains arrived and found one person still clinging to the wreckage. The *CG-38523* had been directed to the *Pelican* by a Coast Guardsman ashore via radio, their visibility severely hampered by seas breaking over the bow. After picking up the survivor and the body of a woman, the Coast Guard continued to search the area for two hours. They then departed for Montauk to seek aid for the survivor. They later returned and searched for several hours, along with the *CG-36516*, but with no success.

The capsizing was not reported to the Coast Guard until Ditch Plains got a call from the Park Police at Montauk at 2:15 p.m. At 11:50 a.m., the Ditch Plains Station received a distress call notifying them that a small outboard with three persons onboard was in need of assistance in Napeague Bay. Boatswain Curles and two crewmen went to the town dock at Montauk and got underway with the motor lifeboat *CG-36516* and made a search of the area. By 2:00 p.m., the crew had traced down the source of the information and found that the boat had made it safely to the dock, but nobody bothered to tell the Coast Guard of this. When reporting back to the Ditch Plains Station, they learned of the *Pelican* disaster. They immediately started the twelve-mile trip, making the best possible speed, and arrived on the scene at about 3:45 p.m. Boatswain Curles complained that he had been called away to search for a boat that had already landed safely.

Mr. William J. Friedel of East Moriches, Long Island, was aboard the *Pelican* with his son, his brother and his sister-in-law. Mr. Friedel, thirteen-year-old Richard and the brother and sister-in-law were fishing near the bow of the boat. "We were under the deck and I don't know how we got out from under," Mr. Friedel said. "When we surfaced I called to Richard to swim clear and kick off his shoes then, when the boat stayed afloat, we swam back to it and clung as best we could."

Mr. Friedel had all he could do to keep his head above water as he was weighed down by a rubberized coat and high-topped work shoes, which he was unable to remove. The waves were smashing into the group trying to hold onto the capsized vessel. His brother and sister-in-law were lost. Young Richard, who had participated in Red Cross swimming classes, was able to get and pass out several life jackets. In so doing, Richard was able to save his father.

Another father and son were not so lucky. Angelo Testa Jr. of Patchogue managed to grab his father, but was unable to hold onto him in the rough seas.

An emergency first aid station was set up at the Montauk Yacht Club. Ambulances had to buck their way through a tremendous traffic jam as those with loved ones aboard jostled with the weekend holiday traffic on the narrow road to Montauk. The highway was blocked six miles back from the point. People were abandoning their cars and setting off on foot.

The excursion boat *Bingo II* picked up the Friedels along with several other survivors and brought them into the Montauk Aid Station. Coast Guardsmen and troops from the 703rd Anti-Aircraft Battery at Camp Hero searched the beaches Saturday night with no success. Among those saved were the twenty-three-year-old mate, Robert Scanlon, and the one man who had sense enough to wear a life jacket for the duration of the voyage. Scanlon stated that the disaster had come without warning. Among those who remained missing was the skipper.

Witnesses to the *Pelican*'s departure from the Fishangri-la at Montauk on Fort Pond Bay claimed that the boat was overloaded, but party boat captains present claimed that charter boats of the same size often carry many more. The number of life jackets aboard seems to indicate that the captain was in the habit of carrying an even larger crowd. He was required to have one life jacket for each person. Newspaper accounts reported "at least 54 persons on board." Of these, only 25 survived, making this the worst marine disaster on Long Island since the war. The "54" figure came up because the captain had told the mate that was the total count. Later, when a count was made of those supposed to be onboard, it was discovered that there had actually been 62 passengers aboard, along with the crew of 2.

By 10:00 p.m. on that disastrous day, the 215-foot *CGC Tamaroa* was ordered to proceed to Montauk to coordinate Coast Guard efforts as on scene commander.

The search for bodies continued for several days. The *CGC Yeaton*, Coast Guard eighty-three-, thirty-eight- and thirty-six-foot vessels participated, along with Coast Guard, Navy and Air Force aircraft. The small craft came from Moriches, Shinnecock, Block Island, Eaton's Neck and New London to assist. Communications truck T11067 and Coast Guard Auxiliary mobile radio units NM3SK and NA3CC arrived and rendered considerable communications assistance.

CG Board Of Inquiry Report 8 OCT. 1951 on the Pelican II

1. At 11 A.M. Capt. Ed Carroll decided to return. It was at this time that engine trouble was experienced. It would seem that only one engine could be made to run, thus accounting for the slow return towards port. She was also headed into the wind until she rounded the point, at which time the wind and waves were pounding the vessel on the starboard side. This caused the passengers to crowd the port side causing a list to port. Two successive seas capsized the Pelican.

2. On Sept. 7, the Board inspected the hulk and made measurements of the deck space available for passengers. They determined that the wooden structure was of sound material, but if she had been subject to Coast Guard inspection, she probably would have been permitted to carry no more than 20 passengers.

3. It was further found that the Captain had grossly overloaded his vessel and that he had failed to distribute the weight (passengers) to trim his boat, he did not keep proper track of the weather and he erred in bringing the vessel in too close to shore where it was caught by the rip tide. He could have made a wider swing into Block Island Sound.

4. The board commended the rescuers, civilian, Coast Guard Auxiliary and Coast Guard working under "extremely adverse conditions" for their work in the rescues. They noted that the 64 persons were thrown into rough seas fully clothed, with little or no wreckage to cling to and no life jackets. They noted that the hull was very slippery and had virtually nothing to hold on to. Only two had managed to hang on to the hull. They further noted that if it weren't for nearby vessels, all would have probably been lost.

5. The Board noted that the Coast Guard needed better facilities at Montauk harbor. [Indeed, a few years later the Napeague

station was floated with great difficulty to Star Island in Montauk Harbor, where it reopened on October 1, 1955.]
6. It was close to 4 miles from the station to the CG boats docked in the harbor. The commander of the 3rd CG district ordered a study of how to improve the Montauk response time.

U.S. Coast Guard regulations were put in place following the *Pelican* tragedy to prevent such an event from reoccurring. As a result, today vessels carrying more than six passengers for hire are certificated by the U.S. Coast Guard under federal regulations.

The *Pelican II* was eleven years old. She was built in Brooklyn in 1940, hull #239733 by Wheeler, originally named *Bell Buoy.*

Some weeks later, after the derelict was towed into Montauk, patches were applied to the damaged hull and transom and it was towed across Gardiner's Bay to Sweet's Boatyard in Greenport, Long Island. After a week on the ways the wreck was moved to a corner of the shipyard for storage. She gradually fell apart until the area was cleaned out to make room for condominiums on the old shipyard property.

THE TALE OF TWO LIGHTSHIPS

Lightships, along with lighthouses, service ships and aids to navigation, were run by different government agencies through the years. The year 1823 saw the first lightship anchored outside of a harbor in the ocean. The U.S. Lighthouse Service eventually evolved and lasted until 1939, when President Franklin Roosevelt reassigned the unit to the Treasury Department, which made it a part of the U.S. Coast Guard.

Lightship duty was usually dull and boring, although occasionally it was dangerous and frightening. These ships were targets for large vessels and if the oncoming vessel did not see them in time, they were run down and sunk, often with loss of life.

At 4:00 a.m. on June 24, 1960, the cargo vessel *Green Bay* was outbound from Port Newark, New Jersey, with a load of general cargo for India and East Africa. It was a foggy night and the ship was headed for the Ambrose Lightship on her way out.

The master had been running various courses looking for the pilot launch. When the launch was located, the pilot left after taking a radar bearing on the Ambrose Lightship. The captain did the same with the radio direction finder. Both bearings agreed, seventy degrees true. The pilot estimated from his radar that the other ship was three-quarters of a mile away. The lightship was sounding the foghorn and the flashing beacon lights were working.

The lookout on the bow of the *Green Bay* estimated that he heard the lightship's fog signal three minutes before the impact. He notified the bridge by telephone and the captain turned ninety degrees to the starboard. As the light became intense, he realized that his ship was closer than he thought. He immediately went into reverse, but it was too late; he struck the lightship with his bow, amidships. The lightship heeled over about fifteen degrees and righted when the cargo carrier backed away. A quick check aboard the Coast Guard vessel revealed that she had been holed and the engine room was flooding, which soon killed the generator, plunging the ship into darkness. The order to abandon ship was given. The crew of nine left in an inflatable life raft, paddling by hand to escape the suction as the ship went down. Their oars were tied down to prevent their loss when launching. At about 5:30 a.m., the crew was located and picked up by a motor lifeboat from the *Green Bay*.

The skipper of the cargo ship was blamed for the accident because he was proceeding at excessive speed of 7.5 knots in zero visibility. He considered his radar as inoperative, even though the pilot experienced no difficulty with it. Old-time skippers were not quick to embrace and trust radar, which appeared for civilian use after World War II ended in late 1945.

The lightship that was struck was on station in Ambrose channel while Ambrose was at St. George, Staten Island, for routine maintenance. She was one of the relief lightships that was used. Her designation was *Relief, WAL-505*.

Visit us at
www.historypress.net